Jan-Erik Andersson
LIFE ON A LEAF
My House as a Total Artwork

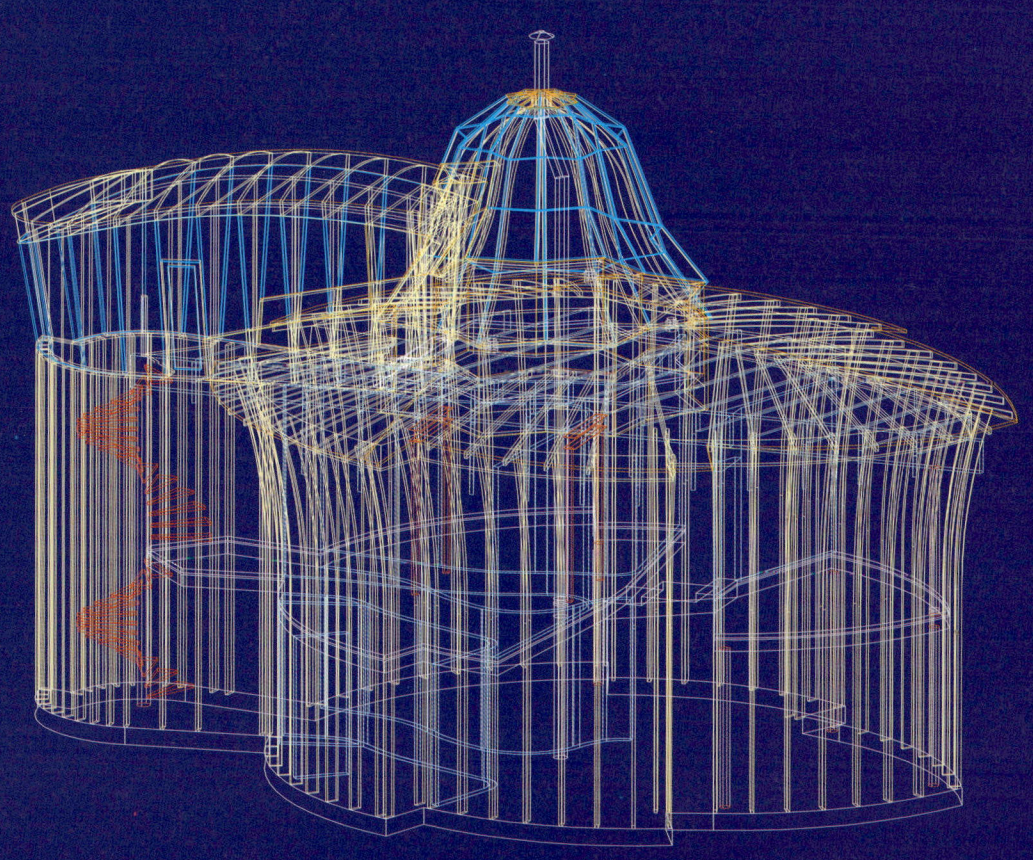

To Liisa and Reijo Joronen
for making the house project possible.

Translation: Kirsti Knox. The stories: Katja Brandt and Robert Powell
Design: Marjo Malin
Photos: Cover: Vesa Aaltonen
Vesa Aaltonen pp.: 10, 13, 20–21, 24, 40–41, 50–51, 67 (2), 68, 90
Matti A. Kallio pp.: 26, 31, 48, 53, 54, 65, 66, 75, 82, 97, back cover 2/3, 3/3
Robert Seger: p. 185 outdoor pictures, cover portrait

All other photos: Jan-Erik Andersson, unless otherwise mentioned.
Published by: AraMER
Print: Nord Print, 2014
© 2014 MER. Paper Kunsthalle for this edition.
© 2014 Jan-Erik Andersson for this edition.
Contact:
info@merpaperkunsthalle.org
jan-erik.andersson@anderssonart.com

ISBN 978 94 9177 553 6
D/2014/7852/233

This book project has been made possible with the support of a.o.:
Oskar Öflunds stiftelse, Academy of Fine Arts, University of the Arts Helsinki, Frame Visual Art Finland

Contents

Introduction 11

Afterword

Erik XIV and Karin Månsdotter 19
Why build a house in
the shape of a leaf? 22
War on "good taste" 23
Art or architecture? 27
Iconic space 29
Iconic windows 29
The house as a forest 32
Sound as an ornament 33
Environmental art 36
Karin Månsdotter and the snails 46
Pehr Kalm 60
The blue ferry 70
Hidden in the Prow 74
Living in an image 77
A ship as a metaphor 78
Loans from nature 83
Living in a nest 86
To live or not to live
– in one's own head 86
Why are there not more leaf houses? 88
Where are we? 96

The Theory Book

The inner room 101
Art Nouveau – Living as an adventure 105
Life on a Leaf, Art Nouveau
and modernism 110
Towards spirituality 111

The house and nature 115
Veronda 115
Shaw 120
Aalto and Le Corbusier 121
Minimalism and nature 122
Ornament as a building's soul 125
Adolf Loos 125
Ornaments of modernism 128
An artist as a genius 131
Postmodern ornament 134
Ornament today 136
Lack inside a building 140
A building as an ornament 141
Surface, structure, ornament 144
Inside and outside 145
Conclusion about ornaments 147

Diary

2001–2004 153
2005 154
2006 155
2007 159
2008 164
Technical Information 178
Invited artists 179
Rosegarden Art & Architecture 184
The house presented in exhibitions 187
References 188

> "Architecture is not simply a platform
> that accommodates the viewing subject.
> It is a viewing mechanism that produces the subject.
> It precedes and frames its occupant."
>
> Beatriz Colomina, 1994

Introduction

It may seem odd to start a study about a leaf-shaped house with a quote from Beatriz Colomina analysing the architecture of one of the key figures of modern architecture, Le Corbusier. In this short paragraph, she does, however, establish the reasons why it is important to create and try out alternative ways of living: this "viewing mechanism", i.e. a house, also "produces" and "frames" its inhabitant.

Colomina detects a connection between Le Corbusier's architecture and mass media (film, movement, communication); a house is no longer a traditional shelter from the surrounding world, but acts like a camera by giving its inhabitants' view of the surrounding reality distancing windows or frames. Thus, a house is no longer designed for a particular site, but rather can be transferred, with an identical floor plan and look, to anywhere in the world, and therefore "The International Style" is a more descriptive name for this style than "Modernism" or "Modern" architecture.

A certain coldness or coolness becomes apparent here. Colomina mentions the film *L'Architecture d'aujord'hui*, where Le Corbusier seems to be walking through the house rather than living in it. She continues: "Even the architect is estranged from his work with the distance of a visitor or a movie actor." (Colomina 1994, 250).

The estrangement I feel from most of the contemporary minimalist architecture that now dominates construction in Finland derives from this distance. Many architects design architectural structures as aesthetic objects, objects to look at.

It is not uncommon that users of buildings by top architects are forced to sign a contract where they promise to refrain, for several years, from hanging posters on the walls or bringing their own furniture to the premises; they must promise to keep the doors shut and so on to ensure that the architect's peers may see the building in its original, virginal state. The design of a building is *not* based on personal and individual stories, the most important elements of which are cosiness, warmth, playfulness, visual richness, ornamentation and dialogue with the building's users.

As a result, architecture is considered merely an environment, a stage for a viewer. There is no need for a house to be an active and communicative organism; it is a plain, neutral and aesthetically sanitised background for artwork and other objects that may interest its occupant.

As an artist who grew up among Modernism, I have asked myself one question many times: why do we not see, in the midst of the stylish, yet aesthetically cold, box-shaped buildings, one single house shaped like a flower, hat or leaf? You may think it is a naïve question, but having worked as an artist in the field of architecture in collaboration with architect Erkki Pitkäranta for more than 15 years, and having seen the negative reactions to the mere mention of the idea of building a house based on play and fairy tales, I thought it was a question worth looking into.

So the idea for building a leaf-shaped house, *Life on a Leaf*, was born, and it was also to become the subject of my doctoral thesis at the Finnish Academy of Fine Arts in Helsinki. The seemingly childish questions soon led to more theoretical considerations: where are architecture's boundaries? What role do ornamentation and art play in a building? The purely pragmatic difficulties are perhaps best illustrated in how difficult it is to be granted planning permission for this kind of building in a city environment. It took five years to receive the permission and if I were not an artist, the house would probably never have been built.

In Scandinavia, this cool, almost Thoreau-like modesty, has become a virtue, and now Scandinavian cool is a brand and an ideal for many people. This – perhaps it could be called stylishness – has its own qualities, but the problem is that it prevents other, more expressive, views and energies from prospering. Finland is often seen linked to the honest, nature-oriented Modernism of Alvar Aalto's spirit, yet people often forget that the same country produced Eliel Saarinen's troll-inspired Art Nouveau houses (see images on page 108) and Lars Sonck's magical cathedral in Tampere (1902–07). It is from the latter architects' suppressed and forgotten energy fields that I started my study of living in a leaf-shaped house whose design was inspired by stories, surprises and dreams. A house where artistic elements claim back their ancient role as a co-creator of the architectural space.

The study also became a journey into a collaboration between an artist and an architect where art is not something "glued onto" a building after it is completed, but is instead integrated into the design of the entire building, from its exterior surfaces to its interior design.

I think we need a paradigm shift after a hundred years of Modernism, which took a stranglehold on the entire previous history and "turned" both painting and building. The abstract reverse side of the canvas and the minimalist shed in the backyard have been considered interesting and aesthetically impressive. The emphasis on the abstract exterior, the abstract space as architecture's essence, has turned into a mantra that is repeated over and over again.

Some may object by saying that during the past ten years, numerous expressive, so-called iconic, buildings have been constructed, particularly in countries whose economic and political situation has made this possible, such as Dubai and China. Yet I maintain that despite the fact that many of these buildings are interesting in their forms and even beautiful, the suppression of playful and ornamental elements applies to them too. The building boom has also had negative consequences: neighbourhoods with traditional small-scale architecture have been devastated.

Due to globalisation, there is no longer one single truth and it is thus difficult to make a statement that would apply to the entire world. But from my Scandinavian viewpoint, the Western architectural mind-set still dominates the Modernist heritage.

We only need to look at the new buildings in Helsinki city centre, such as the new Helsinki Music Centre (image on page 15), which is mostly done in various shades of grey and black. Even the public art in central Helsinki has succumbed to this dreariness. There is a conscious line in this protest against the extraordinary, which Jorma Mukala, chief editor of Finnish architectural magazine *Arkkitehti*, expresses in a newspaper interview on what the Guggenheim Museum in Helsinki might look like: "Let Frank Gehry retire… rectangular, box-shaped buildings are in just now" (*Huvudstadsbladet* 9 October 2011, page 8).

But when I look at the urban landscape that Mukala lives in, I can only say that rectangular, box-shaped buildings have always been in. Why is it so hard to grant permission for something that is expressive and imaginative? It would only really concern a few houses among millions.

This critical, humble view is valid in other countries too. It is still difficult to apply humour or representational elements to buildings. This is demonstrated, for example, in the critical views on the new Stedelijk Museum in

Bruce Goff: *Ford House*, Aurora, Illinois, 1947–50.

Amsterdam, which looks like a bathtub. Critics in the leading newspapers were upset. Michael Kimmelman in *The New York Times* said:

"…entering an oversize plumbing fixture to commune with classic modern art is like hearing Bach played by a man wearing a clown suit." (Kimmelman 2013)

Christopher Hawthorne in *The Los Angeles Times* agrees, and in order to justify his negative attitude even more, he says he finds the building not expressive enough!

"Mels Crouwel dubbed his new addition to Amsterdam's Museumplein the 'bathtub,' a fitting description for such an oversized, antiseptic and mismatched design."

"If there were some humor in the design, some flash of levity to cut through its blinding perma-sheen, Crouwel and his colleagues at Benthem Crouwel Architects might have pulled the whole thing off…but there is nothing of the Claes Oldenburg spirit in the final product, no giant bath towel hanging crisply from the facade with the Stedelijk logo stamped on it like a monogram." (Hawthorne, 2013)

The critics think that these buildings symbolise the wasting of money that is considered typical of the years before the current economic crisis, and thus they can be used as an argument for a simpler and more minimalist style.

We should, however, steer clear of such arguments. Fantasy-filled and ornamented buildings can be made within a budget, as shown for example in projects by Rosegarden (Jan-Erik Andersson and Erkki Pitkäranta), featured on pages 184–185. The eco-friendly *Cumin* (1997) cowshed was completely made of recycled materials, and the *Gerbera* gardening school (1998) done on a budget similar to that of a box-shaped house of the same size. The budget for the *Life on a Leaf* house was based on generating savings by leaving out anything that the family does not need, such as a garage, sauna and basement, and taking advantage of the concept of recycling in the interior design. The total floor area is 147 m² including the Bluebell tower, which is not heated in the winter. It is not a huge house by today's standards in Finland. Our view also means that we have a frugal lifestyle and we can do without any unnecessary objects. We usually describe our house as a maximalist house where a minimalist life is led; it is a total work of art and "complete" in itself. It does not need to be redecorated at regular intervals.

I also think that people need something fantastic and out of the ordinary in their lives in order to be able to go on. When we can afford it, we will build something extraordinary. We need these monumental buildings.

Meanwhile, we are heading for a future where biosciences, recycling, local production and caring will be increasingly important. We need new concepts that not only lay an ecological foundation for construction, but also create a spiritual environment based on nature's forms. The connection to nature should be embodied in the design of buildings too.

The *Life on a Leaf* house I designed with Erkki Pitkäranta is a study of what this future architecture might look like. It should not bring us to minimalism that strips off all "irrelevant" elements from buildings. Quite the opposite: to create an environment where people can live in interaction with nature, we must take into account the significance of comfort, imaginative surroundings and caring individual freedom.

However, even in Finland many houses have been built in recent years that are testimony to this interest in fantasy and playfulness, e.g. Olavi Koponen's detached house *Gastropod* (image on page 141) and Ilmari Lahdelma's Maritime Centre *Vellamo* in Kotka (image on page 145).

And even on the microlevel, outside the official architectural discourse, there are interesting initiatives. The artist Marko Kaiponen produces performances at construction fairs that are a protest against the high cost of housing. He and his wife Riikka have built their house entirely using recycled materials such as old hay poles and skis.

The gap between what a top architect is willing to design and what the customer wants is often wide, sometimes insurmountable. There was a notable example of this in Finland. The owner of Biolan, a large international company that processes manure, wanted to build a new headquarters with a thatched roof. No top architect would undertake such a project. It was claimed that a thatched roof would be a step backwards, a step that could not be taken by any architect who toils forward! So the owner ended up designing the building himself with an engineer. The interior features large logs as tree trunks and other rustic elements that very few top architects would go near. But the owner finds this a warm and humane space.

Yet these views are not only found in Finland. I remember when I was invited to give a lecture at Carleton University School of Architecture in Ottawa; the lecture series was called *Unboxed* and artists, e.g. Vito Accondi and Lucy Orta, gave their views about architecture. The lecture went well and I told the audience about the Rosegarden projects. Then at the reception a professor came to me and said, "You know what, Jan-Erik. It is very interesting that you actually get commissions, but you should know that that is exactly the way we tell our students not to do architecture." To which I replied, "I know!"

Architecture has, at the theoretical level, enveloped itself in a hermetically sealed space where it is hard to be in contact with other views. For instance, there are many architects who would not consider the *Life on a Leaf* house as architecture. This is why I feel a need to confront prejudices and rigid theoretical and aesthetic views that prevent artists, architects, artisans and buildings' users from collaborating on equal terms and employing imaginative sources of inspiration and innovative forms of expression. The *Life on a Leaf* house, this book and the installation with videos about the house and the construction process to

LPR Architetcs: Helsinki Music Centre, 2011.

Marko Kaiponen, Riikka Käppi: Detached house, Toivakka, 1995 –.

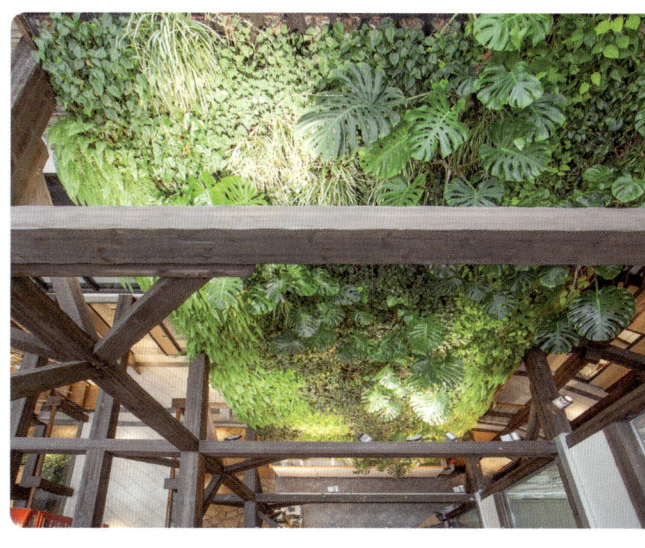

Kariniemi/Vuorinen: Biolan headquarters, Eura, 2010.

be exhibited in galleries and museums are my contribution to the debate.

But, of course, everything is in a constant motion, and just before this book went into print, I received two parcels. One contained the book entitled *Building as Ornament* by Dutch architect Michiel van Raaij (nai010 publishers), which means that the themes I discuss in this book are finally reaching the international architectural discourse. The other contained another book, *Total Design – Architecture and Interiors of Iconic Modern Houses* written by professor George H. Marcus (Rizzoli 2014), which features 18 houses. Marcus is an associate professor at the PENN University, and he has written several books about architecture and design, among others about Le Corbusier and Louis Kahn.

To my amazement, The *Life on a Leaf* house is featured among "...masterpieces of modernist design from the Arts and Crafts movement to the twenty-first century, all concieved as complete works of art, inside and out." The architects who designed the other houses in the book include Charles Rennie Mackintosh, Gerrit Rietvelt, Ludwig Mies van der Rohe, Eliel Saarinen, Alvar Aalto, Jörn Utzon and Daniel Liebeskind.

The house is the production part of my doctoral thesis *Life on a Leaf – Iconic Space. My house as an architectural artwork.* (*Life on a Leaf – Rummet som ikon. Mitt hus som ett arkitektoniskt konstverk*). It was approved in 2008 before the house was completed. The theoretical section was published in Swedish in PDF only and can be found on www.anderssonart.com/leaf.

This book consists of three parts: the new text, *Afterword*, where I discuss the completed house, the *Theory book*, which includes the texts I wrote for my dissertation between 1999 and 2008, and the third part, the *Diary* where the planning and building process is shown as a collage of images. A text version of the diary can also be found in the Swedish and Finnish versions of the dissertation. The three parts can be read as independent texts, which is the reason why all three parts partly deal with the same themes, so some repetition is inevitable.

The theoretical section of my original dissertation also includes *Teoriboken 2*, which features some architectural projects I have done with Erkki Pitkäranta, and discusses some premises for the artistic details in the *Life on a Leaf* house; this section is not included in this book.

Spread among the theoretical texts the reader will find the five stories which I wrote to inspire the design of the house.

It is worth mentioning here that the doctoral degree is granted in recognition of artistic work; the implementation of the house project in my case. Instead of following the academic research tradition, the theoretical texts are rather my personal journey through the theory of architecture and art as well as a more profound discussion about the questions raised during the building process. For instance: why could one not live in an image or in a sculpture? Why could a house inspired by stories and representational forms such as a leaf, bluebell or a Brazilian ferry not be called architecture? Why are there not more houses shaped like a flower, hat or shoe?

It must be stated here, to make sure not to upset any reader who is Modernistically inclined, that the aesthetics of the *Life on a Leaf* house are not exclusive, as is the Modernist tradition. It is instead open and inspired by renowned architects and artists, such as Kurt Schwitters, Le Corbusier, Antoni Gaudí, Bruce Goff, Konstantin Melnikov, Hundertwasser, Archigram, Will Alsop and Rem Koolhaas, as well as the Swedish children's book author Elsa Beskow.

I do not mean to imply that everyone should start building leaf-shaped houses, but I would like to widen the theoretical framework for the concept of architecture. This study aims to create a theoretical background for architecture that is more expressive and based on natural forms. The current architectural discourse is dominated by a vast number of texts that advocate a more rational attitude.

Yet more important than the theory is proving that a functional house can be built around these ideas. It is vital to seek new means of integrating art into our built environment, not as objects hung on walls but as part of houses' structure and appearance. The *Life on a Leaf* house is our laboratory where we can examine how ornament and other artistic elements may now be applied to the interior as well as on the exterior. We updated these elements by inviting some twenty artists to produce art in the house's structures. It made the project harder, longer and more expensive than it would have been otherwise. To many, the long process depicted in the images in the Diary might be proof that one should not undertake a project like ours. I will say, though, that building the house and particularly seeing and experiencing the outcome has been a journey that I have enjoyed. Well, mostly.

Our experiences can, however, be used in producing expressive architecture economically. The appearance of our urban landscape is mainly a result of *aesthetic* selections.

For the most part, the description of the house's ecological dimension, concerning energy usage and heating solutions, has been left out from this book. It should be clear to everyone that we need to build using eco-friendly and energy-saving methods, and these questions are widely being studied now. A short report on how the issues concerning terrestrial heat and recycling were taken into consideration when planning the *Life on a Leaf* house can be found in an info box at the end of this book.

This study emphasises the psychological and aesthetic dimensions that are often overlooked when discussing construction and sustainable development.

AFTERWORD

Erik XIV and Karin Månsdotter

It's autumn and the blue colour abandons the leaves of the trees and disappears up into the sky, turning the leaves yellow and the sky deep blue. A strong wind moves along Vita Bergen in Stockholm, where August Strindberg stands painting. The wind hurls the leaves in spirals into the air. The restless atmosphere is suitable for painting, not for writing. Strindberg brushes away the dancing leaves with his paintbrush and a few droplets of paint fly off and land on a leaf. The paint seems to give the leaf extra energy. It's thrown further up in the air and is caught by a strong gust which carries it eastwards, towards Finland, towards Turku. The city towers up like a grey, silent wall of stone against the Russian empire. A part of Finland, the godforsaken and lost part of the Swedish kingdom. Strindberg sees the leaf disappear, then returns to his reverie of canvas and paint.

The great walls of Turku castle tumble away when Erik XIV outlines her contours with a light hand on a dirt-coloured slip of paper. She is so beautiful, so soft, with a voice that creates music in his head. There is no drawn line that can equal his memory of her naked body when it shivers in the chill of the morning. But the drawing, despite its clumsiness, makes her presence real to him. And the very activity of drawing provides a moment of release from the disturbing thoughts that form like clouds in his mind at times like these, storming those insensitive walls. At moments he can smell her skin as she emerges from bathing in the sea, but it is soon replaced by the smell of dank stone, sweat and wood that surrounds him, filling his body with relentless fear. He will never see her again. Looking out through the barred window to the far side of the river provides no peace. She lives there. Even from here he can distinguish the small human creatures, ant-like in the distance, impossible to control. One of them might even be her, Karin Månsdotter.

Erik XIV looks out through the prison window and sees a leaf that has reached higher than the others, twirling outside the bars, beyond the glass pane. Suddenly it is stuck flat against the glass, like a herald for the mild and weak, its strong veins forming a geometrical pattern. He puts aside the piece of charcoal he's been drawing with, and reaches towards the window. With his forefinger he draws out the contours of a heart around the shape of the leaf where it clings on the outside. He bends forward and gives it a kiss.

The surface of the leaf seems to come alive. The veins turn into small paths, the dark flecks into houses, the colours into fields and meadows. He sees a little house in which he and Karin are hiding, far from the fortresses of power. The house takes its shape from the leaf and melts into the scents and shapes of the air and woods around it.

Then the storm unfurls itself over the landscape and lashes of rainwater grasp at the leaf on the prison window. The leaf loses its grip and is thrown once more into the wind, which carries it over the River Aura to the far shore. There, it drifts gently down into a quiet valley in front of a wooded cliff.

Why build a house in the shape of a leaf?

Having lived in the *Life on a Leaf* house with my family for five years now, I think I am ready to analyse the completed building. Despite the wind hurling the leaf this way and that in the story above, our house became a perfectly "normal", functional house – if we put aside the fact that the floor plan is shaped like a leaf and a Brazilian ferry is colliding with a bluebell on the rooftop!

It became a small house for a small family. Art is not paintings on the walls here; art is a window shaped like a water drop, an opening in a wall in the form of a needle, a poem on a door, a laminated digital photograph as a kitchen worktop and a sound installation that reacts to the changes of wind and light outdoors.

So why build a house that is unique, complex, figurative and based on narratives, when there are so many reasons speaking in favour of a traditional house with rectangular windows and white walls? This kind of house is often cheaper to build and it would be easier to fit in ready-made tables, cupboards and other pieces of furniture.

There was, however, one argument that gave me the energy to tilt at windmills during the long process. It was made by a professor of architecture when I first revealed the plans for the *Life on a Leaf* house. He claimed that we would not feel at home in the house! I simply could not stomach the idea; nobody would decide where and how I want to live for me!

There were other reasons for my ignoring any warnings and deciding to build the house. The most important was the desire to see the house as an outcome of my own dream and not aesthetic systems created by other people. To venture outside mainstream architecture, to a place where fairytale figures, playfulness, surrealism, fantasy and surprises live. To study living outside the box.

This interest has been essential in my collaboration with the architect Erkki Pitkäranta, and has resulted in not only interiors and permanent installations, but also *Cumin*, an environmentally-friendly cowshed for 50 cows in a shape of a cumin seed, designed with cows' psychological welfare in mind, and *Gerbera*, a gardening school extension in the shape of the flower.

We (and their users) saw these buildings as visually stimulating and functional solutions, whereas they were considered marginal, even unwelcome newcomers by some architectural standards. This was why we were extremely motivated to study the subject further. The house in the form of a leaf was a natural step forward.

For us, the building projects are an expression of new ways of interacting and crossing borders to discover something new and surprising. As an artist, I approach reality from the realm of intimacy, details and ornamentation, whereas an architect would approach it from a different angle: from geometry, repetition, capacities, masses, materials and light. These two worlds seldom meet on equal terms.

Working with Erkki Pitkäranta in our company Rosegarden Art & Architecture has been an important experience in this respect, and it has proven that integrated collaboration is viable. The result is not a compromise, but a creation that we both find surprising. Our collaboration is based on our shared belief in the importance of stories and narratives. They have formed mankind's history. Historical buildings, or at least the ones in which any considerable amount of discipline, energy and money have been invested, tell stories through sculptures, works of art and ornamentation; stories that generate new life in the environment. This art element has been in an organic relationship with architecture's structural elements since the dawn of architecture. It was only in the 20th century that architecture came to be seen primarily as something abstract, such as building masses' relation to each other. At the same time, the art element was dissociated and it emerged as replaceable paintings and sculptures.

During the past decade, however, there has been a revival of interest in a comprehensive view, and many so-called "iconic buildings" have been constructed. Other forces have also appeared within architecture. Energy efficiency and ecological living have become established in the mainstream architectural thinking, which also affects the aesthetics of buildings. Yet the legacy of Modernism, interest in "space per se", the empty space between walls and light, are still taken for granted as the truth, and this often manifests itself as leaving ornamental elements out as redundant.

The *Life on a Leaf* house was designed with these Modernist values in mind, but we agree with Louis Sullivan, the architect who institutionalised the slogan "form follows function", in that a house's soul is only expressed by its unique ornamentation. We use art, humour and figurative forms open-mindedly, and thus test the limits of architecture. By planning a leaf house, placing it in the world and observing the reactions it provokes, we can reveal these limits in a fascinating way. The house project, though, has not been confined to a restricted dialogue about the relationship between architecture and art, but rather has expanded into a wider social discourse about issues such as an architect's role as a judge of taste, personal freedom, architecture's role in attracting tourism, town planning and demolition of ornamented wooden houses.

As an artist, I always knew that the house for me and my family would not be a traditional closed house, but a house whose communicative dimension would embrace the outside world too. This is obvious in many ways, one being the invitation to 20 artists to produce art that is integrated in the house's architecture. The house also uses visual and figurative means to communicate with passers-by and thus draws from the expressive and imaginative tradition of Finnish Art Nouveau. We should not forget that even though Finland is now marketed as a country of the Scandinavian cool, it has a deep-rooted expressive and narrative tradition.

Finnish architecture is now dominated by a very minimalist and rational view of construction and human environment. An individual's opportunities for realising his or her unique dream house are very restricted in a society whose aesthetic judgment, even concerning the colour of the exterior walls, is controlled by architects and museum specialists through authorities. How will we live in the future? Will ecological requirements for the construction business, set quite justifiably, provide architects with more excuses to focus on minimalist architecture that would consider artistic elements, ornamentation and humour superfluous or even childish?

The *Life on a Leaf* house was built and this book written because I think we will need these particular elements if we are to create sustainable living environments in the future.

War on "good taste"

Executing the house project turned out to be more difficult than we had expected. When the first plans of the leaf-shaped house were ready, I asked a professor of architecture to give his views on them. He explained that houses have their own "language" and that the house we had designed did not speak this language. Rather, it was an image, and nobody can live in an image! He also said that Pitkäranta, being a professional architect, should stop me from building the house.

When I earned a doctoral degree at the Finnish Academy of Fine Arts with the house years later, it was obvious that the house had been a problem for the official architecture community throughout the building process. One of the opponents, professor Juhani Pallasmaa, wrote in his statement that he could accept the house if I had called it a work of art, but my description of it as an *architectural work* of art was an issue to him. Pallasmaa thought that we should acknowledge the fact that the traditions of art and architecture are not the same. Architecture's function is *not* to

> produce artistic work that is out of its context, the way visual arts do, but to create a framework for the complexity of human life and horizons of interpretation and meaning of the world, life and individuals themselves. Architecture, thus, turns our eyes from its own world of form and expression to our environment, to the world and individuals themselves rather than providing us with products of artistic experience. (Pallasmaa 2008, statement)

Pallasmaa could, however, recognise "broadmindedness, courage, determination and perseverance" in the project, and accepted it.

I also faced numerous problems when I was applying for a planning permission. The process would have been relatively painless had I agreed to build the house in a new area for single-family homes tens of kilometres outside Turku city centre. But since I wanted to gain maximal visibility for the house, I had decided to build it as close to the centre as possible. However, the plots available were all surrounded by other houses so that my house would have needed to meet certain aesthetic criteria concerning issues such as the pitch of the roof, exterior material and colour. This would not have been suitable for the *Life on a Leaf* house.

Eventually, exceptional planning permission was granted and we were able to build the house on a beautiful plot in a park area provided to us by the City of Turku where there are no other houses nearby. If our premise is that a house must suit its surroundings, then this place is perfect. The concept is, though, completely opposite to the original idea of having the house simply "materialise anywhere" among other houses. Now the house is located in traditionally beautiful surroundings, which maximises its aesthetic characteristics, not in contrast to any other houses but by communicating with the nature around it. From an artistic viewpoint I might have preferred to meet "normal architecture" head-on, but since my project also studies how nature can be introduced, little by little, into a house's interior through cultural elements, the place is actually ideal. I have to thank some of the architects in the city planning department and politically appointed officials in the local planning authorities' office for the exceptional permission.

As an artist I find it hard to understand the sharp boundaries between what is architecture and what is not. In visual arts one can choose any means of expression, and the range is infinite in contemporary art. Why would a building be detached from the visual realm and be seen first and foremost as a functional object? The dimension that an architect gives to a building is aesthetic more than anything else. Even though most architects take functionality into consideration, they mainly talk about aesthetic values, really: building masses' proportions, how beautifully the light falls indoors, the texture of materials and so forth.' If we are honest, functionality is, at the end of the day, a problem for engineers to worry about.

A famous example of the primary role of aesthetic values is Le Corbusier's *Villa Savoye* (1928–29). It was nearly destroyed in the 1960s because nobody could or would live in it because it was anything but functional.

Many architects want to keep architecture as clean and abstract as possible, away from the "irrationality" of visual arts. Contemporary architects seldom underline the importance of ornamentation or artistic elements in a building, despite the fact that they often apply ornamental elements in one way or another. These austere aesthetics are supported by a range of statements, often given as eternal

truths, such as a clean, unadorned surface is "timeless" or "leaves room for one's imagination".

A clean surface is hardly neutral, though; it, too, has a visual function. It "speaks" its empty language and has an effect on us both in our private spaces and out in the townscape. Moreover, there are many whose thoughts and imagination require stimulation in order to flourish.

Another argument I hear all the time says that one gets "bored with figurative elements so quickly". In my experience, a floor with figurative patterns that are executed properly and professionally will retain its freshness for just as long as an abstract surface.

After having lived in houses from various periods and various styles for fifty years, I have come to question a large number of the eternal, often theory-based, truths that architects have come up with.

"The good taste" in our townscapes is mainly determined by architects working within planning committees and boards. It is obvious that central areas in towns and cities need planning, but what about areas of small houses? Are we not the best judges of how we want to live? If someone prefers to live in a house shaped like a hat or a leaf, should this not be just as acceptable as living in a box-shaped house? Could houses representing different aesthetic values not be built side by side? Should we not have our say about what our houses look like; about their shape, colour, materials and landscaping? This is, of course, largely a question of context. In some countries the regulations are vaguer and give individuals some leeway, whereas in other countries they are stricter. There are very few places, I think, where architects like to see houses shaped like umbrellas, cakes or flowers being built. In Finland at least, the aesthetics that form the basis for town planning rely on repetition and uniformity. Houses in a block must resemble each other; a block must be an aesthetic unit. There is a conceptual superiority when harmony is used to describe this uniformity and is contrasted against the discord of fragmental impression that is the result of all houses being different. If the *Life on a Leaf* house is considered an artistic research project, then an important part of the research must look into and analyse what happens when it meets society. Who reacts and why? How and where is one allowed to build?

Art or architecture?

Many architects would say that the *Life on a Leaf* house belongs to the realm of art, but how does the art world see it? The artist who produced some of the artwork for the house, professor of sculpture Jyrki Siukonen, would disagree. He does not think that the house is very unusual, despite the leaf-shaped windows and other similar details. "You still eat your dinner at a table and you have rooms with doors, even if the walls are curved." He showed me his latest article, which discusses Gordon Matta-Clark's building cuts and the Merzbau project by Kurt Schwitters. Compared to these two, the *Life on a Leaf* house rather appears to belong to the architectural sphere.

I must admit I mainly agree with Siukonen. The *Life on a Leaf* house is not challenging from the viewpoint of visual arts really, even though it can be seen as an enormous sculpture, and art is integrated in its architecture in a complex manner: we have features such as a sound installation and a video work in the floor.

It is in architectural discourse that the house tests the invisible boundaries passed down by tradition. But what does it feel like to live in the architectural *Life on a Leaf* total work of art? Which of the thoughts that the house has managed to provoke could provide the art and architecture discourse of the 21st century with tangible ideas? Before we step inside, we should have a closer look at one of the project's core concepts: the house's iconic relationship with nature.

Nature as culture in the Life on a Leaf house

A building's relationship with nature and its surroundings is very complex. Most people want huge windows so that they can see outside, yet we still build our houses as shelters against the deadly nature. In this framework, a white cube is the most logical concept. There are exceptionally few rectangular forms in living nature. A white cube not only symbolises our distancing ourselves from nature, we can also *feel* this distance indoors. In this respect, the Modernist white boxes are the pinnacle of progress.

A lot of early 20th century philosophical and artistic thinking is reflected on the glossy walls of the white cube. Nature was likened to chaos and it was thought to be on a lower level than abstract geometry. The roots of this philosophy date all the way back to Plato, through Classicism and the Enlightenment. The architect Adolf Loos (1870–1933) thought that the future would be like "the white walls of Zion", and Kandinsky, along with some of the foremost scientists of his day, rode on a triangle's edge towards an abstract and spiritual future. Mondrian eschewed the colour green in his paintings and sat with his back to the window so that he could avoid seeing the green vegetation outside. Let's hear from Kandinsky's wife Nina:

> *I will never forget Piet Mondrian's visit to our apartment. It was on a glorious spring day. The chestnut trees in front of our building were in blossom and Kandinsky had placed the little tea table in such a way so that Mondrian, from where he was seated, could look out on all of their flowering splendour. Mondrian, of course, insisted on taking a different seat, so as to turn his back on nature (Herwitz 1993, 119).*

Even the new transparent steel and glass structures that came with new technologies were considered to have spiritual content. The architects Bruno Taut, Hans Scharoun, Hermann Finsterlin and Walter Gropius belonged to the secret Crystal Chain (Gläserne Kette) group in the early 20th century; to them, glass was a spiritually tinted symbol of future, even a symbol of a more democratic and transparent society.

Modernism's relationship with nature is, of course, more complex, and many Modernist architects made interesting attempts to connect with nature in novel ways. I comment on these in the Theory Book, where I briefly discuss the approach of Alvar Aalto, Le Corbusier and Tadeo Ando to nature.

By opening walls, building them out of glass and letting light along with surrounding nature inside, Modernism aimed at a more direct experience of the environment. But a relationship with nature through an enormous single-surface window is not that simple. At first one might think that these big rectangular windows allow for an uninterrupted connection with the environment. Yet Beatriz Colomina, an architectural historian, demonstrates that a Modernist window actually alienates; we see the environment like tourists do, from behind a camera. "The picture window works in two ways: it turns the outside world into an image to be consumed by those inside the house, but it also displays the image of the interior to that outside world" (Colomina 1994, 8).

This reasoning brings us directly to the core of the *Life on a Leaf* philosophy. In order to avoid alienation and the sense of a camera's presence, Pitkäranta and I took Art Nouveau's architectural philosophy as our starting point. Both Art Nouveau and Arts and Crafts were movements that sought to find a deep connection to nature through buildings' idiom of forms and symbols such as round shapes, paned windows, asymmetrical structures and figurative ornamentation inspired by nature. However, we are not interested in simply imitating Art Nouveau as a style but rather in applying its conceptual content.

Iconic space

Our premise is that the house should be a shelter – even on a psychological level – yet simultaneously reach out to the environment. In contrast to Modernism, with abstract building mass that symbolises distance and a breakdown of tradition, the *Life on a Leaf* house can be seen as analogous to nature. Human psyche is surrounded by a shell that is neither of nature nor a house in the traditional sense. A variety of artistic elements were applied in the *Life on a Leaf* house to gradually introduce the transition from the nature outside to the mental "space" people experience indoors. I usually talk about nature's "gradual transition" into the house.

These elements are figurative, as opposed to Modernism's idiom, which is based on abstract elements. This is a good place to introduce readers to the concept of "iconic space" that I have been developing during the project. It aims at describing the sense that (possibly) forms in our consciousness as we experience the figurative ornamentation and figurative architectural elements found in the house, such as the leaf-shaped floor plan or windows shaped like a leaf, heart, mouth, bell or a water drop. In addition, we study the ornamental role of sound with an indoor sound installation that reacts to the changes in wind and light that occur outdoors.

This aesthetic framework helps the house to fulfil its aesthetic function in a satisfying way even in surroundings where vegetation is scarce; this is contrary to the Modernist cube, which, in fact, depends on the surrounding nature to provide it, through contrast, with strength.

In aesthetic terms, the *Life on a Leaf* house is an open project. It does make use of Modernist elements too, as seen in the rectangular floor to ceiling windows on the ground floor. Yet they differ from the typical late Modernist windows – which often cover entire walls – in that they are only 40 centimetres wide. The idea is to create an impression of light filtering between tree trunks in a forest. We also want to leave enough wall space between the windows so as to avoid the feeling of being too exposed to the outside.

Iconic windows

In the Theory Book, I describe the difference between living in a Modernist house and in a late 19th century Arts and Crafts house. The latter employs various elements, e.g. patterned curtains and nature-inspired wallpapers, to "bring" nature indoors gradually. In order to create a similar, albeit stronger impression of transition we have used iconic forms – stylised leaves, water drops, hearts and bells/mouths – in most of the windows. The largest and possibly the most imposing of these windows is the one at the front of the leaf. It has been shaped as a leaf with an axis that expands from floor to ceiling. It does not, however, replace a wall as a typical Modernist window would. It opens up from bottom to top, flanking a load-bearing steel "Greek column", the surface structure of which looks like a flower stem, and closes in at the top of the window. The window has been divided into twelve smaller sections, the framework of which clearly marks the fact that we are indoors and not outside in any illusory sense that a wall-sized window might lead us to believe.

Looking out through this kind of window is different to looking out through a rectangular window, in that your gaze cannot help but follow the shape of the window frame, which is based on the forms found outside. The frames do not frame, but "cut out" parts of the environment. Focusing the gaze towards the outdoors thus becomes a gradual process, a certain kind of mental exit. The environment is observed in the same way as if you were outdoors. There, for example, the surroundings are seen through branches or from behind big rocks, and the branches and rocks form "a frame" for the line of sight.

Another example can be found in the kitchen, where a drop-shaped window is located above the sink. We made a conscious decision to position the window so that when you look out through the bottom part, which is also wider, you can see a stone covered with moss about a metre from the exterior wall. Through the top part, you can see a hillside with some trees whose branches filter the evening sunlight in the summer. The apple sculptures in the garden, by the environmental artist Trudi Entwistle, are located so that they cannot be seen if you stand directly in front of the window. Aesthetically, the scene resembles Japanese gardens. Nature is brought into the house gradually with the help of the stone, which can be considered an aesthetic object, detached from nature, and the drop-shaped window leads it into the kitchen visually by "cutting it off" from its surroundings. The chain goes on: its cultural and completely artificial end point is reached at a designer lamp, placed near the window, which has exactly the same drop shape as the window. The lamp is one of the very few furnishings that were specifically (because of its shape) bought for the house. It is near the curvy concrete wall and there is a bench underneath so that we can sit under a drop-shaped lamp and look at a drop-shaped window.

We can also see these windows as iconic symbols or images that float in between the external environment and the consciousness of those inside the house. They generate, as I described earlier, their own mental "space". Perhaps "float" is not quite accurate. Unlike the rationally neutral rectangular shape of "normal" windows, the form of iconic windows is a result of artistic contemplation. Referring to Immanuel Kant, who is discussed in more depth in the Theory Book, we could say they are free forms with no other function. An art element, which really is a drawing of the windows' profile, can thus actually penetrate the wall and create a connection between the interior and the exterior. This gives the feeling that nature is brought into the house gradually. The core of the house's philosophy is also to display the various ways that "free" art elements communicate with its tectonic elements, i.e. the structure that holds the house together.

The relationship between a building's exterior and interior has fascinated architects for centuries, from the architect and theoretician Frederick Kiesler's dream of an endless house where exterior walls become interior walls, to several iconic buildings of the 21st century where the exterior surface has an entirely different idiom from the interior. The *Life on a Leaf* house shows us one solution to this "problem".

Elsi Borg with Otto Flodin and Olavi Sorta: *Lastenlinna*, Lastenlinnantie 2, Helsinki, 1948.

César Manrique's house, Lanzarote, 1966.

The house as a forest

In the space of "gradual transition", we are, in a sense, more "out in nature" than when standing in front of a large Modernist window. This aesthetic is carried on in the iconic floor plan and curvy walls. Perhaps not instantly recognisable, the leaf as a shape is constantly present in the subconscious because the floor plan is designed as a stylised leaf. The leaf can be sensed also when looking up at the 14-metre long glulam beam that runs along the middle of the ceiling. Green laminated veneer lumber beams grow out from it diagonally towards the outer edges of the space like veins of a leaf.

A house made of cubes with rectangular openings forces our gaze to follow the straight lines, then stop at the corners, follow the straight line again until it reaches the next corner or opening. This is the case even when there are openings for imagination in the form of windows, works of art and decorative objects. Being, moving and letting your eyes wander about in a space like this is completely different to doing so out in nature.

The *Life on a Leaf* house follows nature. The leaf-shaped floor plan ensures that moving through the house is like walking along a path in a forest. We have also created a number of "tree trunks" inside the house; variations of Greek columns, the central pole of the spiral staircase and the floor to ceiling chimney of the heat-retaining stove.

Because of the curved shape of the house, your gaze is never stopped by a corner as happens in a cube. Here, your gaze always meets a vertical pillar, a "tree trunk", the side of which lets in light from outside, and your eyes then move on to the next pillar. Outdoors, our gaze moves from countless details at various distances towards infinity. Even though we live in systems of boxes, we do not move along straight lines, and our natural way of moving and seeing is less restricted and less systematic.

It is almost impossible to come across right angles and rectangular forms in nature. The architecture in the *Life on a Leaf* house supports our natural way of moving and seeing via its floor plan and iconic windows. It is in sharp contrast to what a box-shaped space can offer us.

The *Life on a Leaf* house does not provide us with the kind of "shelter" that a white cube does; a static and geometric form that is a "proof" of our distancing ourselves from the "chaos" in nature. Instead, we have a space (in the broad, spiritual sense) that reminds us of the "shelter" that woods can give us. When we stop in woods, we can feel safety embracing us. Perhaps we could define it as a safety created by beauty, yet we can see and sense the infinite nature between trees and branches.

In his conversations with the architecture critic Hal Foster, the sculptor Richard Serra explains how the bent sculptural forms he has used and studied for years display an important element of architecture in this century: "…the demise of the right angle; there will be more curvilinear, more open spaces that are swift, that float, that change velocity, or otherwise nuance time. (Foster 2011, 234).

Sound as an ornament

In my attempt to define the concept of iconic space, I dealt with the space that is created by employing iconic forms as architectural details, windows and the floor plan. An equally important element is the traditional ornament, the theory and complexity of which I discuss in the Theory Book. In the Life on a Leaf project, I focus on ornamentation that refers to nature and on sound as an ornament. I have studied the latter extensively in collaboration with the sound artist and professor Shawn Decker.

When we are about to enter the house, we can look up at the roof edge, where three small "Mickey Mouse ears" rotate around a thin bar. This is a wind sensor and part of Decker's work. A couple of metres underneath, there is a small white capsule, which is a light sensor. Much in the same way that the iconic windows act as cultural elements in bringing nature indoors gradually, these sensors communicate changes in the nature outside into the house. Changes in wind and light are not transmitted directly to the 30 small loudspeakers located in the house, but the impulses are relayed through Decker's computer system, which manipulates them so that they resemble sounds created in nature. The outcome is a series of short creaks that have become part of our everyday life.

Sound's ornamental characteristics have been studied in many ways. Oskar Fischinger (1900–67), for instance, replaced wave-shaped soundtracks with ornamental patterns along the edge of strips of film in order to create "pure" sound. Decker has worked together with nature to produce an ever-present, ever-changing system of quiet sounds that form a transparent constellation in the house's space. Wind and light are not ornaments per se but play a part in the creation of an ornament.

We can also see a poetic dimension in the soundscape surrounding the house. Gaston Bachelard's book The Poetics of Space contains a paragraph where he, in his apartment along a busy street, feels that the roar of Paris sounds like the ceaseless murmur of flood and tide. It is clear that traffic cannot replace real waves, but this emphasises the power our consciousness has as a creator of our mental states. This, of course, requires us to have recollections of real waves (Bachelard 1994, 28).

The soundscape of the Life on a Leaf house is somewhere between urban culture and forest-like park, where birds, foxes and hares live and where the blowing wind rattles the trees. When it is windy, there are the exciting, added sounds of ropes chinking against masts of sailing boats moored in the small nearby harbour.

The road in front of the house is not very busy yet; we can clearly hear every single car driving by. Possibly the most thrilling sounds come from the city harbour, where the Turku to Stockholm ferries arrive and leave every day. When we are in the bluebell, the winter garden on the second floor, we can see the ferries' funnels, and when the wind blows from the right direction, we can sense their smells and scents; we can even hear their various signals, sometimes the announcements over the loudspeakers. All this shrouds us with the ambience of a journey, and thus enhances the house's association with a vessel. To me, this brings back strong memories, because my father was a sea captain and I used to spend a lot of time aboard ships and at different ports.

Behind the house there is a rock wall that broadcasts its full range of sounds from the swish of treetops to the trickling of the water down the stone when snow is melting.

The acoustics in the house are excellent. A conductor who visited our house tested this by singing in different places and he said that sound is much softer in our house than in box-shaped houses, where sounds are flung between the opposing walls.

Quite surprisingly, it is nearly impossible to tell which floor sounds come from. Sometimes we run up and down before we can locate a ringing phone. We designed the house deliberately so that sounds carry from the ground floor up to the computer studio on the second floor. The sleeping loft was left half-open to ensure that sounds can be heard there too. We live and even sleep in an open space. We like it; it is easy to communicate with the other members of our family. Naturally we have the option of having some privacy: we can sleep in Marjo's study or close the door of the bluebell or our son Adrian's room.

A mother who visited the house with her two children was surprised that she could not hear the children running on the first floor. That is one of the benefits of a 40-centimetre thick concrete floor.

Nature as a metaphor and ornament

Before we enter the house, we should stop for a moment to have a look at the exterior. The house looks very different when seen from far away, from the street, than it does from the garden. The bluebell conservatory on the

roof is almost five metres high and looks really imposing and massive compared to the rest of the house from a distance, yet when you approach the house, it shrinks little by little and finally disappears altogether when you reach the entrance. Immanuel Kant, analysing the experience of the sublime, described the optimal distance for looking at pyramids in order to properly experience the sublime. There is no optimal distance for looking at the *Life on a Leaf* house. We could say that entirely different houses emerge.

Let's study the relationships between the visual, iconic elements more closely. Regardless of the figurative elements such as the leaf, bluebell, heart and mouth, the house is certainly not an "oneliner" – a term coined by the architectural theorist Charles Jencks to describe "bad" architecture. A hot dog stand in the shape of a hot dog, for example, refers to something outside itself too unequivocally.

I wanted the surreal jumps in scale in various parts in the house to cause aesthetic clashes, which would lead to different associations and emotional charges. The leaf-shaped floor plan is gigantic compared to an actual leaf. The leaf-shaped window is small compared to the leaf-shaped floor, yet enormous in comparison with an actual leaf. The bluebell is gargantuan compared to a man, but tiny in relation to the leaf of the floor plan. The water drops are, quite realistically, in proportion to the house's leaf-shape but enormous compared to real rain drops. Moreover, the leaf shape of the floor plan gets volume when we move upward, which adds to the cubic capacity and complicates the aesthetic expression and creates associations with a huge ship. The computer studio on the second floor, "the Brazilian ferry", is the only element whose scale is more or less realistic, excluding the bluebell if it is seen as a lighthouse. The shapes of mouth and heart in the windows could be seen as taken from a giant, who also positioned the leaf window at the front of the house.

All these elements can be considered as parts of the house's ornamentation because its expressive form ensures that its character, as a whole, is ornamental. Equally, it can be seen as an enormous sculpture. For this reason, it is not necessary to place ornaments on all exterior surfaces, and I have, contrary to the first sketches, limited the ornamentation to those surfaces where the house meets the sky and the earth, i.e. the traditional places for ornamentation. The ornamentation on the main building's base was inspired by the idea of integrating classical ornaments into an element found in the surroundings. I have used the palm leaf motif in my earlier work, and as it happens to be a common motif in classical ornamentation, it was natural to have it as the starting point. The local material was right there: there are ferns at the edge of the forest, which are some of the oldest species of plants still in existence. As ferns look like leaves of palm trees, the ornament became a synthesis of the two, and since the "serrated" floor plan divides the base into clear sections, it was natural to alternate the palm leaf/fern ornament with another ornament: a giant hogweed. This is a tall plant that was originally used in gardens but now must be removed because of its toxicity, especially if it grows near children. When the foundation of the house was laid, all the hogweed was dug up, although now it lives on as ornaments.

The ornamentation at the base is classically severe on the front, but at the main entrance and around the stem, the palm leaves and hogweeds have gone through a chaotic "gene manipulation" and the ornaments go crazy.

To counterbalance the base, there is an ornamental frieze under the roof edge consisting of spades, hearts and fir trees. I have applied these forms in my earlier art projects, and at least for me, they portray the Finnish soul: dig hard for some love under a fir tree! Only a coffee cup is missing. The motifs are laser-cut in aluminium and stove enamelled blue, red and green. They are attached to the wall with an 80 mm gap, and the roof edge protects them from the rain. Yet even this is not quite the way it should be: on one side of the house the motifs are the right way, on the other they are upside down.

Environmental art

Let's spend a bit more time looking at some artwork outside before we walk into the house. We asked some twenty artists to produce works of art for the house's architectural structures. To ensure that there was room for surprises, we asked them not to take the house's aesthetics into consideration, but to follow their own instincts. Still, many works are comments on nature and the house's role as a mediator between nature and culture. The environmental artist Trudi Entwistle, for example, designed the area around the house. She planned two slopes in the backyard that gradually bring nature closer to the house. On one slope there are three apple-shaped bench sculptures, the "windfalls". We can lounge on them and stare at treetops and clouds. Entwistle thought that nature should remain as it was; no flowers or shrubs were planted, we only cut the grass so that we can walk on the patios.

She designed an oval area of grass in front of the house, between the apple trees, that was kept from the plot's former life.

In front of the main entrance there is a two-piece work of art by Frank Brümmel. One part is a concrete table that we use as our dinner table in the summer. The table top is covered with lines that describe bees' dance in the air when they show other bees the way to food. The other part is a black and yellow concrete surface outside the entrance; its ornamental design resembles a beehive's structure.

Hanging up high from a branch is a bird house by Joonas Mikola. Birds are actually not able to live in it

though, because it is made of concrete and the opening is just a painted black circle. Huotari makes these bird boxes as 3D graffiti and hangs them from locked chains under bridges and similar places.

Let's go inside! The house turned out to be a total work of art during the process, and we intend to keep its appearance the same for as long as we live in it. Our idea was to integrate all the works of art into the architectural structures, not as separate pieces attached to walls. The only place we have traditional works of art is the loo on the first floor. Art has reclaimed its pre-Modernist role as an integral part of the building's general architectural impression. There are, nevertheless, many significant differences. One is that the artists were particularly asked not to adapt their works to the house's overall aesthetics. Instead, each work supports the concept of a complex mosaic of aesthetics that is characteristic of the completed house.

We will not be refurnishing the house every autumn just for the sake of change. The change is already in the art, ornamentation and architectural details. There will always be a new viewpoint, a new combination of details – and we will have time for other things. This has an ecological dimension, too.

When we enter the house through the main entrance on one side of the leaf's stem, we are first met by a mirror that covers the entire opposing wall. Adolf Loos, among others, used mirrors to create illusory openings on walls. We took this a step further. The mirror creates an illusion of a second entrance, where the nature outside is reflected; it forms an "un-world". The effect works especially well when we sit at Frank Brümmel's concrete table in the garden and look at the opening through the open main door. The world appears to continue, as a copy made by the mirror, on the other side of the house and we can see a similar family doing the same things that we do.

The mirror reveals another world, too – that of poetry: on the inside of the main door there is a welcome poem for the house written by Robert Powell. It can be read on the mirror as the text is printed as a mirror image on the door. The poem can also be read on the house's website.

The stem of the leaf is big enough to be an entrance hall. When you look to the left, you will see a spiral staircase that leads up to the upper floors. The ultramarine staircase was specially designed for this space and the steps are welded onto the steel pole inside the structure. The pole, the diameter of which is that of a fully-grown tree, is one of the six "tree trunks" on the ground floor. The others are the floor to ceiling chimney of the heat-retaining stove, three load-bearing concrete pillars that were cast in situ and the white steel pole in the front part of the house.

We will not go upstairs yet, but let's have a look to the right, where we can see a grey concrete wall in the middle of the house. This has been left unpainted, giving the impression that we are standing beside a rock wall. It was also inspired by Modernism's love of "pure material".

To make the wall livelier, I used the same technique as I did in the ornamentation on the base. Plastic cones and mouldings were attached to the casting moulds and left depressions in the wall that form ornamentation in the shape of dandelion seed heads. This motif was not premeditated like the one on the base; rather, I was inspired by nature. When we were casting the wall, the air around the house was full of dandelion parachutes. At the time, I was looking for a means to include in the ornamentation the little round holes that would stay on the wall after the moulds were removed. They became parts of the dandelion seeds.

The heart-shaped opening in the concrete wall leading to the kitchen looks like a door to a cave and enhances the feeling of standing at the foot of a cliff.

Even though the entire ground floor is one open plan space, excluding the bathroom and maintenance room, the curvy wall in the middle effectively blocks taking in the whole ground floor in one glance. If you look into the kitchen through the heart-shaped doorway and let your eye continue to the living room, passing along the kitchen units and appliances, you will see a range of vertical elements: narrow windows, narrow wall segments between the windows and concrete pillars. Together they form a forest of tree trunks, which the light from outside filters between, just like in a real forest. The load-bearing concrete pillars were cast in drainpipes that we lined with a plastic fluted sheet to make them look like weathered Greek columns. They are meant to be a comment on 18th century Romantic architecture, the period when castles, viaducts, bridges and other constructions were built to look like they were ruins from an earlier era.

The light plays its way indoors in a similar manner on the other side of the building when we let our gaze glide past the corridor flanked by the concrete walls. In the middle of the kitchen we have a table consisting of two hexagonal nuts that I designed for this area. Both tables stand on castors so that they are easy to move.

The surface of one table is inspired by the burning core of the earth and is computer cut acrylic that shows flames. Among the flames, there are round engravings with snakes, flies and insects cast in lava. The lava was collected around César Manrique's house in Lanzarote, which was built in five volcanic bubbles. The table top is attached to a large stump.

The theme of the other table is space. Yellow acrylate is set on the surface to represent the sun, and stones collected in various parts of the world orbit the sun. The table stands on a little house made for wine bottles.

There are two lamps on top of the tables, both designed by artists: Pertti Toikkanen's hat lamp, which is made of organically grown wheat that has been forced into form and dried, and a waste basket turned upside down with a small figure of a cleaner on the edge, made by Kari Juutilainen. Both lamps were left unpainted so that together with the concrete walls they are a neutral counterbalance to the colourful kitchen table.

The laminate surface on the worktop is a piece by Karin Andersen. She has worked on the themes of zoomorphism and produces digitally manipulated images. In this work, she depicts herself as a hybrid of an animal and a chef. The figure flies around in space, surrounded by eggs, ketchup bottles and kitchen utensils. It is fantastic that by placing an object onto the worktop it automatically becomes part of Andersen's work of art. Being able to see our friend who we otherwise do not manage to see very often also added a dimension to our mental space.

But we are not going into the kitchen; we stay at the heart-shaped doorway. If we take a look to the right, we can see a corridor curving between the concrete wall and the bathroom wall. The other wall displays ornamentation; this time it is two showers dribbling water bubbles down to the floor. The corridor invites us to see what lies at the other end of the "path". Stepping into the living room is like stepping into a clearing between two rocks in woods. Suddenly you are met with an opening that is six metres high, where light pours in through 40 centimetre wide, six-metre high windows that arch inside on the top, and the black-green-white ornamentation on the floor that was inspired by my story:

Karin Månsdotter and the snails

Karin Månsdotter is walking on the shore, back and forth in the wild patterns of increasing hysteria. The autumn wind is already so cold that she would normally need to cover her head. But since her head feels overheated by thoughts about the transience and randomness of existence, it gives her a sense of freedom and oneness with nature to let the wind bite at her skull and numb her mind.

Her beloved, King Erik XIV, is still imprisoned in Turku castle on the far side of the water. Uncertainty about his fate has changed her life and created new, desperate habits. Several days a week, when the weather permits, she rows over to the island opposite the castle, the one that the local inhabitants call Hirvensalo. From there she can see the tower of the castle and imagine Erik sitting by one of the barred windows, perhaps watching her. Sometimes, standing there, she imagines flying up into the air and meeting Erik on one of the clouds in the clear blue sky, where they make love joyously and weightlessly. But then the cloud becomes ice-cold and she drifts alone back to earth, like snow.

Now, back in reality, she walks in the cold autumn wind into a little clearing that forms a protective haven below a steep rocky cliff. She sees something gleaming on the ground next to one of the wild apple trees. Although she knows she should get home quickly before the darkening weather gets worse, her curiosity gets the upper hand.

She leaves the safety of the path and ventures out on the wet ground towards the apple tree. But she trips on a protruding root and falls, gashing her leg and hip on a stone. She screams in pain and loses consciousness. Waking later from pain and cold she tries to get up but can't. Providence, that has given her so much of love and power in her life, now seems to have abandoned her, helpless and alone on the ground in the woods. Time passes, panic grows. This is a road that few people use, and she has no idea when or even if they will start looking for her.

Lifting her head she notices that her white dress has provided a painterly canvas for the red blood as it meets and mixes with the blue-brown wet clay into various shades of umber and autumn. And despite her predicament, in a kind of reverie, she cannot help but reflect on the unexpected beauty of the deep red where it meets the intense white. It makes her think of the beautiful colours of life in the royal court, which she had experienced for such a short intense time.

She has fallen close to one of the apple trees, whose trunk has been turned almost black by damp and decay. There are still patches of grass between the flecks of newfallen snow that are already being stained a dirtier white by the heavy clay on the ground. The green colour of the grass has gained a brilliant intensity against the white of the snow. Near her is a fallen apple, so black that no animal has touched it. The last thing she sees is an army of small black creatures crawling slowly up her torn dress. She had never thought of snails as dangerous, but seeing them now in their hundreds, she loses consciousness and waits for death.

The Artsoppa group (Pasi Helin, Tanja Nisonen, Jukka Perksalo, Marja Springfeldt) performing in the house 2012. Music by John Cage, Terry Riley and Steve Reich.

Every artistic detail in the house is based on a story. This may be a more abstract process behind artists' works, not necessary obvious in the works themselves, or more direct if the work of art or ornament is an illustration to a story. The ornamental patterns on the floor depict what Karin Månsdotter saw just before she died under the apple tree outside the house: some patches of snow on the autumn green grass among the black rotting apples. The visual inspiration derives from the apple orchard in our garden, where windfalls turn black and then decompose into nothing. The floor surface is, indeed, part of the aesthetic concept where figurative ornamentation helps us to bring nature in gradually and where the richness of colours is concentrated on the floor and ceiling, leaving the walls more neutral.

The front living room features the leaf-shaped window. There is a group of couches in front of it and a light installation on the ceiling: 26 different dimmer-controlled lamps acquired from charity shops are arranged in three circles. This installation is a tribute to the lamp shops I used to stare into when I was a child, hypnotised by the light from hundreds of lamps shining in the winter darkness. This is one of the strongest visual memories I have from my childhood. The lamp shades have their role in the house's aesthetics too; they try to evoke memories and often succeed when visitors recognise one of them.

Under the lamps we have an old black table designed by Alvar Aalto. The floor underneath was painted yellow to honour Aalto's Paimio Sanatorium; he used a similar shade of yellow on the floors there to cheer up patients and their families.

If you raise your eyes towards the ceiling, you can see a small bridge that crosses the clearing from one cliff to the other. The bridge's ornamented railing contains the tiny loudspeakers for the sound installation that make barely audible clicking sounds. On the ceiling, we can see the green beams that take their form from a leaf's veins.

As we let our gaze wander around, we can see other works of art incorporated in the structures. Dancing legs penetrating the concrete at the bottom of the bridge by Susanna Peijari; Yuichiro Nishizawa's cut through the wall of Adrian's room in the shape of a fir needle; Alice George's poem, composed when we were painting ornaments on the floor and written on a rolled-up piece of paper, then hidden in a hole in the wall, and Jan-Kenneth Weckman's minimalist line drawings on the stove's plastering. The heat-retaining stove is located in the middle of the house and is its heart. We brought the couches in front of the leaf window from our previous living room, and they are now separated into three parts. The textile artist Johanna Kunelius designed a pattern especially for the *Life on a Leaf* house, which we then printed on fabric, and we had some covers sewn that now envelop the couches. This is one example of the philosophy of recycling that we observe in the house.

You can return to the spiral staircase from the living room either through the kitchen or along the corridor between the concrete walls. It is thus possible to walk – or even run – around the wall in the middle. It is a very inspiring spatial element, especially if there are children in the house; it also bears similarities to traditional Finnish construction methods, since the main buildings on farms were often designed so that you could walk around the middle section.

Now we go to the corridor and open the bathroom door. Where the other walls are minimalist white or unpainted plywood, the bathroom walls are filled with colourful mosaics. Here too, the theme is taken from nature. We stand on a small island in the middle of a sea. The floor is made of green tiles, with the occasional sand-coloured tile on the sides. The island has trees that grow on the mosaics on the walls, and at the bottom we can see the deep blue sea under the yellow sky. The bathroom cabinets are placed so as to seem to hang from the trees; an apple is hanging from one branch, a bird is perching on another. There is a plane in the yellow sky and a red dragon in the water. Adrian was four when we were building the bathroom as relaxation therapy for the entire family after the "serious" work carried out elsewhere in the house. He made a robot that shoots with a laser gun out of mosaics; this we have on a branch too. My father, who was a sea captain, sails with us in a ship beside the bathtub. Marjo designed the area beside the door, and since she is a minimalist, she mostly covered it with black and white birch trees and black sky.

There is a narrow window that stretches from floor to ceiling; we can lie in the bath and admire the stars. An uncovered ventilation pipe takes an extra twist under the ceiling, which shows how easy and cheap it is to change the character of a pipe.

More ideas for recycling: the ochre toilet and yellow washbasin came from a recycling centre and we found the blue bathtub.

After our tour downstairs, we come back to the staircase that leads all the way up to the second floor. At least on a symbolic level, the staircase can be seen as a tree trunk, with steps for its branches. Behind the stairs, there are vertical windows, 20 centimetres wide. These are invisible from the stairs and hidden behind a plywood wall. They go through all the storeys in the house; it is like a gap between two rock walls where the light flows in. The window is an example of a fruitful collaboration between architect and artist, where both can apply their special skills. It was Pitkäranta's idea to place the window here, and proof of the importance that architects attach to light spreading indoors. Beside the windows, there are full spectrum daylight bulbs that create an illusion of summer light entering the house during the dark months. The ornaments on the railing are laser-cut on metal panels. The motif, which is based on plugs and stars, generates changes of light

and shadow that look like patterns found in nature when light is reflected through branches and leaves. The effect helps to light spaces in our imagination and strengthens the impression that we are walking around a magic tree.

Even though I try to use simple pictorial shapes, the railing ornamentation is not quite unambiguous: instead of a plug, one visitor saw a bull's head there!

Now we arrive on the first floor. We see a drop-shaped window with blue frames. It illuminates the corridor that runs between the curvy, lacquered plywood walls like a path, and on to the bridge, which looms in front of the heart-shaped window. The path can be lit indirectly by switching on a series of full spectrum lights that were installed on the timber below the 14-metre glulam beam. When the lights are not lit, the bridge gleams dramatically in the light coming from the living room. When we keep going along the corridor, we can see an Eastern-inspired forest silhouette on one side of the bridge. It is actually a half-open wall of shelves that shelters the loft in front of the heart-shaped window. The heart shape is one of the oldest pictograms found on cave walls. Connotations aside, it is a very dramatic sign, whose soft curves are in contrast with the sharp point. The heart comes from the story that inspired the leaf house. Erik XIV drew a heart onto the prison window before the leaf was blown away.

The sleeping loft floor is about 30 centimetres higher than the rest of the first floor. This means that the bridge slants upward slightly and thus gives going to bed a sense of occasion. It is also easier to get up in the morning knowing that we can slide down along the bridge! In addition, the solution means that the living room underneath is very high and the 26 lamp installation has enough space around it. Sleeping in the half-open room is like sleeping under an open sky. The reference to nature is clearer again: when the night falls, the shell wall looks, from the bed, like the forest outside. Behind it, the green glulam beam dramatically disappears toward the spiral case.

Smaller beams grow diagonally out of the main beam towards the exterior wall. They have leaf ornaments on the sides to cover and protect the daylight lamp technology. Here you can truly encounter the richness of forms, colours, light and shadow – not forgetting Shawn Decker's sound installation, the loudspeakers for which are set in the railing ornamentation. It is an enriching and soothing experience to fall asleep when these sounds mix with the fridge's hum downstairs and other spontaneous creaks created by timber. Occasionally, a mouse may join in the concert.

The ornaments in the railing display Pehr Kalm's legs as he runs to his garden in Sipsalo, only a few kilometres from our house. Kalm, who was a student of Carl Linneaus, established the first botanical utility gardens in Finland in 1757.

Pehr Kalm

It was extremely warm and the stench of the city was unbearable, even though the worst heat of summer was long past. So as to get some fresh air and make a last inspection before the winter, Professor Pehr Kalm had decided to row across to the garden that he had created out on Sipsalo manor in Hirvensalo, an island in the River Aura. The garden was an outlying annex to the botanical utility garden that he, together with Johan Leche, had created near the Turku Cathedral in 1757. After all the problems that he had had during the summer germinating the seeds he had collected in America, it was necessary to carry out the hibernation correctly. Despite all his efforts to protect the plants from frost, he knew that many of them would probably not survive. Yet it was worth the effort.

Kalm decided not to row all the way, but to go ashore by the little village opposite the castle, and then make the rest of the journey on foot. He knew that in the Renaissance the castle had been a residence, modest but still unique and impressive in a poor country like Finland. Now it served only as a prison – and no longer for kings, as before, but for common criminals.

Kalm was an optimist. He believed that by investing in science and education, a better future was possible, even in a country at the periphery of civilization, like Finland. That is why it was important to make sure that the garden would flourish. His vision was that it should be feasible to develop useful plants that can stand this climate, and he had the University's full support to explore new cultivation methods.

Kalm started walking along the road in the woods towards Sipsalo, thinking fondly about the garden's rational, geometrical structure, when he noticed how illogical and organic the route of the winding road was. It should really have been straight – then he'd have saved some time! There is beauty in simplicity, he thought. His botanical utility garden was shaped around a rectangle, a divine geometry that distinguishes us from Nature. Mankind is, after all, the pinnacle of Creation.

He breathed in the scent of hundreds of different flowers and trees. Just then, he was reminded of his physical existence by a pressure in his groin. He had to stop to relieve himself. He stood in a clearing where some wild apple trees were growing, haphazardly directing the stream of his urine to the south, so that the sun, which had just appeared from behind the grey clouds, made it glow strangely. At the same moment he thought he saw an object gleaming on the ground a short distance away. It was not easy to discern, obscured as it was by a particularly thriving stock of giant hogweed. Furthermore, the ground in which it grew had an oddly familiar, human shape – the shape of a woman lying just beneath the soil!

Buttoning his trousers, Kalm pushed into the giant hogweed towards the spot. Using his walking stick to strike at a particularly large plant, he broke its stem and was immediately enveloped by an indescribably sweet and sour odour. His nostrils dilated and he staggered back, gasping for breath. His last sensation was of a rainfall of small, sharp needles shooting from the stem of the giant hogweed, and a liquid that flowed over him in an unbridled stream.

One day my partner Marjo exclaimed: "What's a house without a bridge!"

When I was designing the house with cardboard models, a bridge was one of the architectural elements that I found the most stimulating. Born and bred in Turku, I have always been inspired by the bridges that cross the Aurajoki, which runs through the town. Crossing a bridge, you enter a no-man's land, on your way somewhere, leaving something behind; the middle of the bridge is a kind of a free zone.

The bridge in the *Life on a Leaf* house is an intimate yet theatrical space for Adrian to play in; he can raise his head over the railing and shoot at the villains running around in the living room. It also offers a proper perspective towards the floor ornamentation downstairs. Many visitors have said that they have felt like making a speech from the bridge to those on the ground floor.

The bridge is a fantastic element for stirring the imagination and riding on an emotional rollercoaster. Just think about all the bridges in films and books – bridges where sighs are heaved and kisses exchanged. Martin Heidegger uses a bridge to depict a place's character in his essay *Building, Dwelling, Thinking*. A bridge does not simply connect two places; it also creates a place where the bridge meets the earth.

One end of the bridge is a place for rest, whereas the other forms a small round area around the red load-bearing steel pillars, which can be seen in front of the library entrance. The pillars were originally going to be hidden inside walls but at the last minute we decided to move the wall by one metre, thus cutting off a part of Marjo's room. This allowed us to have a small library, where the wall against Marjo's room houses a bookcase and a metre-high railing protects against falling. At the end of the library, against the exterior wall, we managed to squeeze in a little reading corner, which has a special feature: if you turn your head and look up through the six-metre high vertical window, you can see Turku Castle.

The ornamentation and artistic elements can be seen in their full glory from the bridge and in the library gallery. From "the top of the cliff" we can look down on "the clearing" and the living room floor ornamentation or along the corridor toward the staircase, which stands out against the light from behind. It is like living in a castle, although the house's entire floor area is no more than 147 square metres.

I have mentioned before that we wanted to place ornamentation mainly on the floor and ceiling levels, leaving the walls unadorned. This was partly an aesthetic decision since opposites complement each other, but it also forms a kind of dialogue between Marjo's minimalist and my maximalist tastes. I am interested in this kind of communication between different ways of thinking and experiencing, even on a global level.

The floor on the first floor corridor has a geometric pattern consisting of triangles and squares made of linoleum tiles in different colours. We had the tiles cut using computer-controlled watercutting and then glued them onto the concrete floor.

I chose the pattern and the colours with Matilda Ekman, a design student. The abstract and geometric pattern is one of the elements that breaks with the house's metaphor for nature: the aim is to make different aesthetic ideas communicate with each other, not to follow one uniform style.

We leave the bridge and library and go back to the staircase along the walls bent from plywood. Finnish architects use a lot of plywood, but it normally it has to be as unknotted as possible – and minimalist. True to our alternative views, the walls here and around the staircase are made of cheap knotted building plywood, which has been sanded down and varnished. This gives us nature's own knot ornaments for free. It feels nice to touch the curvy forms of the walls; it is like putting your arms around a thick tree.

On the way back to the stairs, there are rooms on both sides of the corridor with identical doors. They contain twelve little glass panes, which makes it possible for light to enter the rooms from the corridor. The rooms also have windows on two different walls, which helps to create a light filled space in the rooms. The doors were donated by a joinery shop; they had been left over from a renovation job in an Art Nouveau building in Turku.

One of the rooms belongs to our son Adrian. He chose the light blue "police colour" on the concrete floor himself. The room shares a special feature with the entire first floor, in that it has an exterior wall that bends both horizontally and vertically, as well as narrow and curved vertical windows in the leaf's "sawteeth". Combined with the iconic window in the shape of a mouth (or two bells), it creates a unique ambiance.

Green timber beams cross the ceiling and support the roof. Underneath there are dimmer-controlled daylight lamps that shine an indirect light into the room. It is an ideal place to play with small Lego bricks during the dark winter months.

The wall in Adrian's room, standing against the six-metre opening to the living room, is split by a 50-centimetre long cut in the shape of a fir needle. It is covered with glass to prevent sound travelling to the living room. A number of lengths of wire are attached inside the cut that look like real fir needles. The cut is a work by Yuichiro Nishizawa, and is placed so you can see the Turku Castle through it. This is another fine example of what an artwork can be if its idea is present as early as in the design phase. We earmarked the area on the wall for this work, and then Nishizawa sent it in a box by post and we attached it to the hole in the wall.

The other room is Marjo's oasis. One of the conditions Marjo set for the house project was to have her own study that she would be allowed to design by herself. Other than this, she granted me the power of veto over all issues concerning the house's appearance, since it is not only a family home but also a work of art by Pitkäranta and me. We did, however, discuss most of the solutions, and the fact she sanded and painted most of the surfaces ensured that she could leave her minimalist aesthetics visible on their final form.

On entering Marjo's room, you first notice that the green beams turn to white. Originally, Marjo wanted to leave the floor unpainted, the grey of concrete, but since she could not finish it as smooth as she wanted to, she decided to paint it deep red.

The door of the French balcony has a metre-high protective panel. Marjo is a graphic designer and designed it herself. The text UPP PUPU UPP is cut into the black aluminium panel, her comment on the Finnish-Swedish positive "upp culture" that I represent. It is believed in Finland that the Swedish-speaking minority lead happier lives than the Finnish-speaking majority. The Finnish word for a rabbit jumping about happily is pupu.

The communication does not stop there: I replied by sawing an Eastern-inspired harem profile on the façade around the French balcony where it can only be seen from outside and painted it orange!

Just before the staircase, at the end of the corridor, there is the other toilet, which has two functions. We use it at night to avoid walking on the stairs in the dark and it is a technical room with the air ventilation unit and aerial attached high up on the wall.

The loo was inspired by the privies typical of Scandinavian summer cottages. I can remember them vividly from the childhood summers I spent on an island. Often they would have a little window and their walls were papered with posters and pictures from magazines. The wallpaper in our "privy" was designed by Chicago-based artists Burtonwood and Holmes. It is called *Apache* and features an ornamental pattern where an American bomber meets with explosions and flying meatballs. The text "99¢" appears at regular intervals.

Jyrki Siukonen's small collage is on top of the toilet seat. It is entitled *Stuttering Modernist Shit* and comprises the letters KAKKAKAKAKANKANDIDINDINKSKSSKY.

We wanted to have a window in each room, loos included. We also spent a lot of time turning the loos into thought-provoking and philosophical rooms. The form of the window in this loo was borrowed from the architect Konstantin Melnikov's house in Moscow, completed in 1929. The house, which enjoys a cult status now, consists of two cylinders and its façade is ornamented with hexagonal windows. From our loo window you can see nature climbing up a rocky hillside. This gives going to the toilet a dream-like quality at night, especially in the moonlight.

The author outside Kostantin Melnikov's house (1927–1929) in Moscow.

Sitting in the small room with a curvy protruding exterior wall is like sitting in a tiny space capsule designed by Jules Verne. For the floor and wall borders, we made a chequered racing flag ornament from leftover pieces of mosaic.

After closing the yellow toilet door, we are at the blue tree of the spiral staircase again, facing the second floor. Many people might find it strenuous to run up and down the stairs several times every day but it has lots of benefits: it keeps us fit and is aesthetically pleasing.

The blue ferry

The little boy lies on a hill. In the bright moonlight of the Brazilian night the hill is not black but white. His father has disappeared, gone with Alzheimer's into the silence. The boy gazes up at the stars that look different here in the Southern hemisphere than they do in the North. He turns his head 180 degrees and admires the silence that speaks from outer space in the steaming night that smells of hot sand, palm-leaves, decaying wood, and oil from the generator in the village. He remains slumbering the whole night on the sand. In the morning he is woken up by a colibri that has stopped in midair in front of his eyes. Everything is still, safe in ultra-rapid. Today the boy is due to go to meet a teacher who works with the children in the little village on the island off the Brazilian coast.

He sets off, but when he reaches the place where the school is supposed to be, the only thing he sees is a big tree. Then he hears laughter coming from the tree, and discovers a group of children – ten of them – sitting in the branches. One by one they jump down onto the ground, followed by their teacher, a young woman from Sao Paulo who has come here as a volunteer to teach the children. Why yes, the school works in the tree, she says, but we also have a table with benches here next to it, where we can work with paper and pencil. The boy sits down and starts drawing what life looks like in a country that has ice and snow. Meanwhile the other children draw their reality, with colourful fish, turtles and canoes.

After some time the boy leaves school, carrying in his mind images of sun and sand, leaving behind a sheet of drawings filled with black, white, grey and blue. The boy wanders for a long time along the abandoned sandy beach, with the ocean on one side and the impenetrable jungle on the other. He sees no one, except for one man who approaches him wielding a huge machete. But the man passes by without pausing or saying a word, just as a woodsman might back home in cold, old Finland.

The boy reaches a village that has a ferry connection to the next island. The ferry only goes a couple of times a day, and is just about to leave. It's small, made of iron, its deck a rectangular plate on which wooden benches are fastened, just like in a church. Blue painted posts sprout from the deck, holding up a roof. The boy sits down among the other passengers, mostly very dark-skinned women dressed in white. The ferry chugs slowly out from the harbour. The boy thinks of his father, a ship's captain who sailed the seven seas. He remembers seeing photos of his father tarred black, a ritual that was carried out on cargo ships whenever they crossed the equator, heading south. Now, in a way, he feels he's following in his father's voyaging footsteps, but doing it his own way.

The boy wakes from his daydream and discovers that the ferry is not heading towards the next island at all, but out into the open sea, the Atlantic Ocean. He also notices that nobody else is with him anymore. The ferry moves forward, ghostlike, the coast behind disappearing and the waves ahead growing bigger. This was the way that the Portuguese had come when they first arrived in South America. Now the boy is heading on the same route but in reverse, back, straight towards Africa. The little ferry moves steadily onwards, under the huge blue sky.

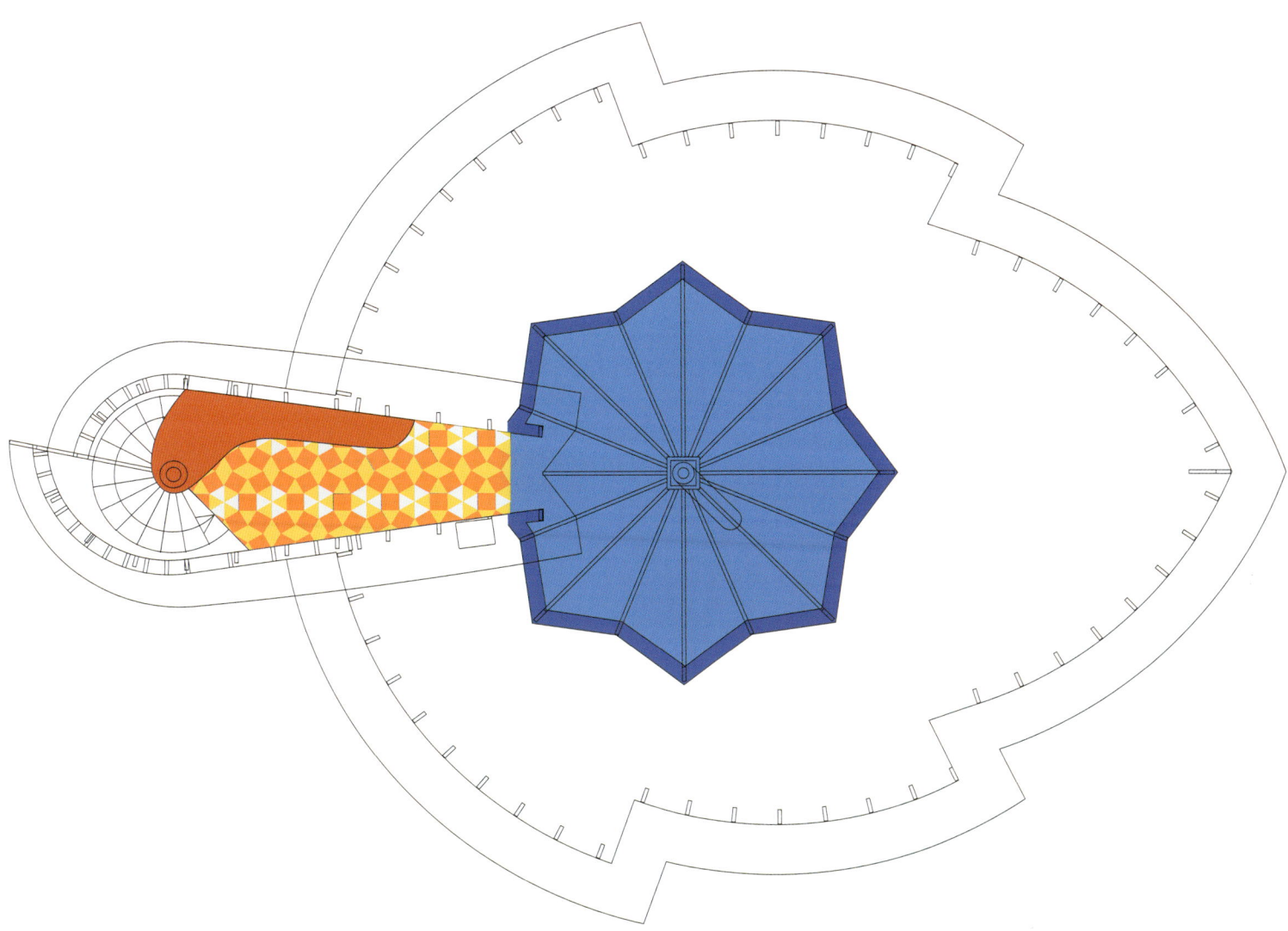

I do not want to give up on the metaphor of nature yet. When we arrive on the second floor, we encounter a blinding light. Most of the wall surface on the top floor is covered with windows. A sense of climbing up a mountain, from the lower regions of caves and dark shadows towards the top, is tangible. Pitkäranta and I have applied the mountain metaphor in our earlier projects in order to create different moods in buildings that are constructed upwards.

The idea to build upwards came from two sources: partly from the English three-storey townhouses, "pieces of cake", that I lived in when I spent six months in London, and also from Gaston Bachelard's poetic view that a house is a block of psychological storeys where, for example, the basement represents the subconscious. The outcome is a house with three storeys, each of which has its own ambiance and where you can find a suitable place for each mood and need.

The idea for the computer studio, though, came from a Brazilian ferry that I sailed on along the coast near Bahia. Its area is only seven square metres, but it is spacious enough for one person and a computer. The room seems bigger because of its peculiar design. Since my head requires more room than my feet, we had the windows installed at an angle so that the room is noticeably wider at the head level than on the floor. This is actually a functional solution: when it rains, the windows barely get wet. The same applies to the main part of the house, "the leaf", since its walls expand just below the roof. This means that the roof edge is nearly a metre wide and protects the walls, windows and aluminium ornaments placed under it.

Two of the studio's windows can be opened and you can step out onto the roof. Take careful steps and you can sit outside the bluebell of the winter garden. This is really living on a leaf!

The regulations concerning insulation in single-family houses in Turku are very strict. All windows must be fixed and ventilation managed mechanically. Yet there has to be an exit on each floor in case of fire. That is why we can have two hinged windows here that also serve as emergency exits. They are indispensable in summer when the studio becomes very hot. I usually open them both to create a real draught. The studio's south-facing wall has no windows in order to keep too much sun from getting in.

Hidden in the Prow

The little boy held his legs tightly together, bending them closer to his body to keep whatever little warmth was left in him. His fingers were white, even though it was the middle of June. But summers in Finland can be cold when the wind comes in from the ice sea in the North. Under him he felt the hard, uncomfortable construction of the little tree boat, hand carved by his uncle. His eyelids fell slowly in time with the rhythm of the waves, and he was lulled into a dreamlike anguish in that little boat, sensing the immense black sea beneath him. He was vaguely conscious of the a mild smell of wood varnish mixed with the steam of the old Seagull engine that slowly, but loudly, moved the boat forward through the narrow coastal inlet.

The boy held his breath to hear the waves better, lapping against the prow of the boat, a quiet churning so different from the waves that hit the boat with a roar and a bang in stormy weather. Here he lies, the son of the sea captain, under the little bench in the bow of the boat. This is his place; he is safe here. There is no need to talk, only to be, with his father steering the boat. The boy looks at his thin white fingers; not the fingers of an old sea dog from the salty seas, alas, rather they are sensitive and very pale. He believes this is because there are so many thoughts in his head that all his blood is needed there: his fingers and toes just have to do without it.

If I could ever build a house, he thinks, I would build it shaped like the bow of a boat. Then it would be a house where I could sleep without nightmares.

But it was summer now and the sky was clear blue. The terrifying school is gone, the one that turns his speech into a jumble of stuttered vowels and consonants, and into a silence so loud that it seems to speak – yet never says what he wants, wants, wants, wants, wants.

Looking up, he notices that his father is wearing a funny white seaman's cap. An ordinary seaman's cap on a captain! And the thought occurs that perhaps his father doesn't really want to be captain. A captain has to make decisions, always know where he is heading, has to sit and eat alone. Maybe he would rather be an ordinary seaman, just following orders. And just then – hey! – there goes the cap up in the air, heading over the water towards land!

His father steered hard to one side, so that the small wooden boat lurched heavily, because he wanted to get his cap back. Luckily the boat happened to be close to land and he and his father went ashore on a small stretch of sandy beach that lay between the surrounding dockyards. The cap had disappeared a little higher up in a clearing near the steep cliffs, and father and son ran after it with little hope of getting it back.

On and on the cap travelled, up the cliff and into some woods. The boy wondered whether it was worth all this effort to get the old, yellowed cap back. But his father continued further into the woods, where walking became difficult. Maybe Daddy needs a new hat, thought the boy, and saw in front of him a huge over-nourished bluebell, whose colour was so bright it competed with the sky. Maybe this could make a new hat for Dad! The boy snatched the bluebell from its stalk and was just about to give it to his father when suddenly they halted in surprise. They had arrived in a clearing, with two blackened shapes on the forest floor in front of them. The shapes looked like grave mounds and were surrounded by giant hogweed plants that seemed to stand guard over them.

On the ground, between the mounds, an object gleamed strangely. Both the boy and his father remained still, breathless, looking. They could feel that this was a special place, haunted yet calm, a solemn place where something significant had happened, maybe long time ago.

On top of the first black mound there was a very large birch leaf. Without thinking, the boy reached out and put the bluebell, not on his father's head, but on the leaf. This is what my house will look like, he thought, a house in which it is possible to make silence speak.

Brazilian ferry that inspired the look of the computer studio. Photo taken in Porto Seguro, 1994.

A bluebell gave me the idea for the winter garden, which is an extension to the computer studio. The stories I wrote to inspire the house's architecture demanded that there be a bluebell on top of the leaf. By designing the glulam beams with a CAD programme, we managed to achieve a bell-like structure resembling a bluebell. In my art work, I have used the shape of a bluebell many times but never on this scale: the bell's top is nearly five metres high. Its structure was a design challenge as the frames of the glass panels are easily damaged by rain. The sensation produced by looking at the surrounding nature and the town's silhouette through the blue-framed window is unique. We are on the same level as the birds building their nests in the trees beside the house. It is wonderful to be able to follow the birds flying around for almost 360 degrees and to observe the movements of clouds, the changing colours of the sky, the moon and light from the stars. It is especially lovely to sit here in the rain and watch water trickling down and forming patterns on the glass panels. Here too, the iconic form of the bluebell has an effect on how nature enters our consciousness gradually.

The bluebell was originally designed as a cold winter garden, but during the construction process it developed into a meditation room with good insulation and double glazed windows. A timber wall on the south-facing surface, which leads to the computer studio, protects the space from the heat of the sun. On sunny summer days it is too hot in the bluebell because there is no ventilation. But on cool, typically Scandinavian summer nights, filled with mosquitoes, when it is still light all night, the bluebell is fantastic. To save energy, we do not heat the room in the wintertime. It is always a magnificent ritualistic occasion to reclaim the room after the winter.

Thoughts on an iconic room

The ambiance produced by the bluebell and the round table in the middle of the room invites you to sit down at the table and try to figure out if a house, the design of which is based on iconic symbols, can create a meaningful mental world for its inhabitants. I doubt anyone would question the fact that the world looks different here. After having lived in the house for three years, we can say, loud and clear, I as a maximalist, Marjo as a minimalist: we love it! It has not been quite this simple for many who are involved in architecture; even during the design phase some voiced their opinions that the house should not be allowed to be built and that we would not feel at home there. And please do not call it architecture.

Marie Antoinette with architect Richard Mique: *Le Hameau*, Versailles, 1783
Salvador Dalí: *The Mae West Room*, Dalí museum, Figueres, 1974.

Living in an image

Of course it is impossible to describe the house's spaciality, intimacy and comfort with the two-dimensional media like photograph or film. Many people who have visited the *Life on a Leaf* house after having seen it on television or in a magazine have been surprised at how cosy it really is. Regardless of how well or badly images manage to communicate the warm atmosphere of the house, it looks good in pictures and on film. This was a surprise to me as I have previously had problems with documenting my three-dimensional art installations in museums and galleries. Perhaps the house works so well in pictures because it is a picture (of a house)!

These thoughts were provoked by a letter from the first supervisor of my doctoral thesis, Professor Kaj Nyman (Nyman 2000, letter). He advised me not to build the house because my family and I would not feel at home there. He explained that houses have their own language, an idiom that *Life on a Leaf* does not represent. Nyman is critical of most Modernist architecture but I do not find his alternative particularly interesting. In his opinion, the best representatives of "houses' language" are farmhouses and the 1920^S Classicism. Nyman thought that *Life on a Leaf* would be an image of a house, if anything, and we all know that you cannot live in a (two-dimensional) image!

I am not sure what he would think of the house now that it is completed, but we who live here know that he was clearly wrong. I would argue that "houses' language" that would make people feel at home does not exist. Architecture professionals have always tried to find a measuring system that would make buildings harmonious and humane. Even in the name of Modernism, many attempts have been made to develop an anthropometric module, a measuring system that could be applied in constructing large yet "humane" complexes. The most famous of these must be Le Corbusier's Modulor. One of its measures is 226 centimetres! It is interesting that Alvar Aalto, when asked about the measures of his studio's module, replied, "One millimetre or less."

Later, in the 1960^S, Aalto was accused of elitism by a group of young architects who wanted to produce functional and affordable architecture for masses. I can understand the desire to build houses and apartments for all the workers needed in various industries, but to claim rational Modernism as the model for "humane living" and architecture with a capital A is quite another story.

The relationship between a two-dimensional image and a habitable, three-dimensional object is fascinating. We could study a surprising topic in more detail: Marie Antoinette (1755–93). Mentioning her in connection with architecture might be somewhat provocative, but those who have visited her *Le Hameau* with an open mind will disagree. There, you must struggle to keep the issue at hand separate from the social injustices and other arguments that taint our opinion of the queen. Marie Antoinette was forced to live a regimented life in the very rationally designed Versailles. Despite the rich ornamentation indoors, its architecture is very severe if we consider it as abstract masses. Even the exterior ornamentation is very spare. Life in the palace was extremely organised and controlled, even retiring to bed had become a public spectacle.

To counterbalance the routine and control, Marie Antoinette decided to create her own domain in 1783, where only her friends were allowed to visit. Le Hameau was only walking distance away from the palace. Among the grottos and cottages, there is a hamlet that resembles a Norman farm, not inspired by a real farm however, although there was one near Le Hameau, complete with a peasant family that looked after some animals. Instead, she asked Richard Mique (1728–1794) to design a realm based on the ambiance in a painting by Hubert Robert (1733–1808), in other words, on a two-dimensional image. In current art parlance, the entire project might be called a conceptual installation. There are life-sized houses in the hamlet, yet some are built on a smaller scale, such as a lighthouse and a non-working watermill. Marie Antoinette used one of the houses as a temporary lodging, while in another she served fresh milk from a nearby farm to her guests in the morning. The constructions represent two levels: one is surrealist works of art, the other habitable buildings. Marie Antoinette proved that it was possible to live in an image!

Another interesting example is the Salvador Dalí museum in Figueres (1974). The entire complex is a mixture of old buildings with new ornamentation (e.g. casts of Catalonian bread) and artistic details, such as eggs and divers on the façade. Amidst this collage of a theatre set, architecture and painting you can find a Buckminster Fuller glass dome.

Due to the museum's hybrid character, it cannot be found in architecture books nor in art books. To me, seeing it was a powerful experience, as it cannot be simply placed in one category or another, which compels visitors to question all preconceived notions. One of the rooms developed from a painting of Mae West by Dalí. You enter a theatrical room commanded by an enormous nose-shaped fireplace. On top of it, there is a painting on both sides, and in front of it there is a couch shaped like lips. The room looks peculiar but it is completely functional. You get the idea when you step on a small stand at the other end of the room: there is a lens through which you are supposed to look at the room. Suddenly the room becomes a two-dimensional image of Mae West's face. The paintings turn into her eyes, the fireplace her nose and the couch her lips. Even Dalí proved that it is possible to live in an image – if you want to!

The image we inhabit is different, though, because it was based on a three-dimensional model on a 1:20 scale. It is living in a sculpture, rather, but I do not think this would tone down Nyman's criticism. If anything, he thinks that design should rely on the relationship of abstract masses to one another, without involving numerous images and iconic elements into the planning. Most architects consider them redundant and dispensable.

Here I would like to point out that several architects and architecture theoreticians, e.g. Owen Jones (1809–74) and Louis Sullivan (1856–1924), emphasised that only ornamentation can give a building its (individual) soul, despite their support for constructive and abstract elements in architecture.

To finish off, I will return to an image. In order to break through, Modernism's minimalist white aesthetics required some assistance. It was a great help that those who founded the movement and those who found it appealing could write and felt the urge to theorise. In the history of architecture, there have always been theoreticians who have been interested in classicist trends, whereas more expressive movements, e.g. Baroque architecture, have not attracted theoretical writers of the same calibre. Perhaps this is down to the fact that the architects producing expressive architecture "feel" rather than analyse their work rationally. Also, expressive architecture uses more direct means of communication, and therefore it has no use for theoretical support.

Le Corbusier published a magazine and wrote books that promoted Modernism as well as his own designs. He retouched his photos to make his buildings (their images) impressively stylish. Beatriz Colomina shows a funny example where Le Corbusier had removed, among other things, a terrace and a kennel in order to highlight the pure architecture.

Anyone who has taken a good look at Modernist, white plastered concrete houses know how quickly and easily they start to look weather-beaten and dirty. Especially in tropical countries where Modernism has been very popular, such as Brazil, there is a myriad of buildings whose large white surfaces have been taken over and cracked by debris and plants carried with rainwater. It is vital to create a printed photographic illusion of white, clean modernity and future. It looks as if Le Corbusier believed that the essence of architecture lay in the sketch and the drawing, not in the actual building.

A ship as a metaphor

Using metaphors, particularly those referring to nature, is common in contemporary architecture. Very few, though, are quite as brave in their unambiguity as Herzog and de Meuron were in their design of the Beijing National Stadium, which was modelled after a bird's nest. There is a great risk of producing a house with just one interpretation, a oneliner.

In his article in Taide magazine, the critic and artist Kimmo Sarje bases his criticism of the *Life on a Leaf* house on a ship metaphor. He sees me as a sea captain's son, who sails the stormy seas between art and architecture. Even though

Pitkäranta and I consider the leaf shape as the starting point for the house, and even Sarje acknowledges this, he still focuses on the obvious bow that is the house's front part. He sees clear associations with a ship's aesthetics in the spiral staircase, bridge and the "cabin-shaped" sleeping loft. He is completely convinced by the 14-metre long glulam beam, which together with the smaller beams form a pattern that, to him, looks similar to a ship's hold. He does not make it explicit, but the connection to Le Corbusier is obvious.

It is rewarding to read analyses about the house written from different perspectives. The subconscious can have many effects and I suspect that very few artists know what they really do. The computer studio on the second floor was inspired by a Brazilian ferry; drawing a parallel from a leaf to a ship is actually not so far-fetched then. Interestingly, this reminds me of Le Corbusier's admiration for big ocean liners, which he thought were the face of the new architecture and exclaimed: "Why are they sent out to sea?" (Le Corbusier 1986, 92).

Our approach to architecture is, on surface, far from Le Corbusier's modular system or the idea that architecture is about "masses' ingenious communication with light", or that "a house is a machine for living in"(Ibid., 95). But if we take an objective look at Le Corbusier's architecture without the context of his writings, we notice that his buildings, particularly those completed after the World War II, have many sculptural features and, surprisingly enough, quite a lot of ornamentation! Many of his projects also have direct references to ocean liners: gangways, crow's nests, curvy shapes and wall-to-wall windows.

In one of the stories I wrote for our house, I deal with a childhood memory of one of the times our family was on the sea in a small wooden boat, and I lay hiding my head under the bench in the prow. I dreamed myself far away as the waves kept lapping. The sleeping loft in the *Life on a Leaf* house really does look like a boat's prow.

Perhaps it is possible to reach very similar outcomes from completely different starting points? Pitkäranta and I based the house on the stories I wrote. In practice this means that if the stories require that we place a bluebell on the rooftop, we will place it there. We do not ponder whether it is good architecture, but whether "it feels good". Still, even if we start with natural forms, these must be functional. The computer studio, or "the ferry", was invented because I needed a study.

Le Corbusier might note that in construction, there is no initial form which the content is then "forced into". His starting point, like that of Art Nouveau architects, was function. Suitable masses are piled beside and on top of one another, and a house's appearance is defined by these masses.

Despite the leaf house's floor plan being predetermined, the house is actually an open space, the interior of which could have been filled in many different ways. Our first idea was to add small wooden cabins to the hall-like space; they could be bought ready-made in a local hardware store and attached to poles, and they could be assembled into a system of bridges. If there was a need for another room, we could simply buy another cabin.

Although our "version" of the interior turned out to be a total work of art that we will not be likely to change, it would be quite possible to come up with other versions and redesign the interior in an entirely different manner. Even the floor plan could be executed in various scales. So, coming from a different starting point, we end up with a building that shares many features with Le Corbusier's designs.

The house can be seen as a small ocean liner where interior walls are made of crude concrete, windows reaching down to the floor, which consists of a huge open space and has a wheelhouse on the rooftop! Kimmo Sarje describes the interior:

The contrasts are more pronounced indoors than outdoors because the space is tense between concrete brutalism and playful ornamentation. The curvy reinforced concrete wall that dominates the kitchen and the living room – reminiscent of 1950^s Brazilian Modernism – challenges the entire Moomin World (Taide 2/2010).

In spite of the metaphors applied by many architects, most of them would not recommend starting points that are too literal or mimetic if a high-quality architectural structure is their ambition. Professor of architecture Antonio C. Antoniades writes:

[…] we have notorious examples of buildings that look like boats, elephants, or hot dogs, or that carry other images, perhaps more universal and difficult to achieve, such as the house with a human face by Minoru Takeyama, the house for an archaeologist that looks like a broken column by Boullée, and the series of houses of ill repute by Ledoux which are phallic symbols. In many of these instances, there may have been an initial humorous disposition, which in itself might have been worth keeping, but in most cases it is a naïve effort at creativity, which, in the absence of anything more relevant, resorted to the gimmicks of literality and visual mimicking. […] Literality has the negative potential to enlarge the crowds of unstimulating, unimaginative people. For this reason, it should be avoided by architects (Antoniades, 175–177).

Stories as sanctuaries for grown-ups

But why should literality's link to a building be prevented? You would think, rather, that it would give new creative and playful energies to a townscape and its inhabitants. I would be happy to move into the houses by Boullée and Takeyama mentioned above. Regrettably few architects devote themselves to examining this area. They are in

"a higher spiritual sphere" and for that reason, this type of design can only be encountered in Disney establishments and cheap commercial environments. Usually their hot dog stands and "fairy tale buildings" are not particularly well executed. Yet I find it hard to agree with Antoniades that "literality degrades imagination" (ibid., 175). After all, it depends on how well the idea is realised and the building is constructed.

There are a lot of complexities involved here that should be examined in more detail: the huge gap between children's happy and colourful culture and the composed and serious culture of grown-ups. Should we not ensure that our everyday environment is interesting and stimulating enough so that we can get rid of all amusement parks?

Comments we have heard from guests include: "Oh, how exciting this house is; children must love it here", or from a visiting architect: "The house would make a perfect crèche." My usual response is: "Perhaps so, but it was designed for grown-ups. Children are normally fine when left with a cardboard box and a frying pan; these are enough to stimulate their imagination."

One of our priorities in designing the house was to prove that grown-ups are content in an environment that offers a more direct connection to fantasy and opens the doors to the areas in our consciousness that were created by stories we heard as children. I believe stories and fairy tales, told in words and in images, conjure up moods in our consciousness. They give us a sense of security that we can return to later in life. I think that a house that produces an iconic space originating from stories and fairy tales can serve as a sounding board and stir an emotional response in grown-ups by allowing them reminisce about these stories or memories and feelings left by them.

Once we invited over about twenty nursery friends of Adrian's, who was six at the time. The following day the children were asked to draw the recollections of the house they remembered best. Most children drew Adrian's Lego bricks and the onion shaped sauna outside the house. Only one child, indeed, drew the actual house. I had been expecting this. Adrian says he would like to move back to the little 50-square metre apartment where we lived before moving into the *Life on a Leaf* house. There, he could fill the entire living room with his belongings. To him, the new house was a little frightening. He does not like being alone on any of the three floors after darkness falls. I am sure that the childhood spent in this house will leave – hopefully positive – emotional marks in Adrian, which he will, I hope, appreciate when he grows up.

When I spoke with the head of the nursery about children's imaginations, she said it may be that many children do not need much support for their imagination, but there are always children who do require this support because of a lack of stimulation. Thus, from her point of view, the stimulation offered by the house, even during a short visit, was remarkable.

Loans from nature

Even if houses are not allowed to look like hats, hot dogs or ships, architects tend to be less critical about borrowing forms from nature, particularly if these forms are not merely copies but used as metaphors. For Antonio Antoniades, however, the Finnish architect Reima Pietilä is an example of how excessively expensive it can be to produce architecture that follows natural forms: "[…] nature uses the law of least energy, whereas one must spend extraordinary amounts of energy to construct the natural looking, irregular forms of the imagination" (Antoniades, 247).

Sometimes you hear architects claim that nature is rational and, given a chance to build a house in the best way it could, it would choose the most direct and simplest method of connecting two points together; in other words, it would draw a straight line.

But if nature is rational, would it not follow the laws of entropy, which state that energy tends to always gravitate towards a lower degree of intensity? From an organised state to a less organised state, i.e. towards greater entropy?

But what does man do? By building and organising, using the sun as the source of energy, organic nature, man included, constantly tries to avert chaos. (This is possible in small sub-systems, whereas in larger systems entropy grows.) It is in our nature to build complex systems. Through evolution, nature continues to build uncountable and different "redundant" variations.

This is why I consider a development towards more imaginary shaped, playful and, at the same time, more complex architecture as a manifestation of our intellectual and human existence.

In many cases, it is more costly to produce a minimalist surface. A lot of money and design energy must be invested in hiding all the architectural details that would otherwise be visible.

Hal Foster discusses this feature in contemporary architecture, which has moved from the traditional Modernism whose main themes were functionalism and transparency, to a variation of minimalism that is very expensive to produce. Foster describes this process in relation to planning of the New York MoMa extension. "Raise a lot of money for me, I'll give you good architecture; raise even more money, I'll make the architecture disappear" the architect Taniguchi is said to have told the trustees. 425 million dollars bought a construction of white boxes where complex and costly technical solutions managed to create large white rooms without columns, which are waste of space, and to lift wall surfaces a few centimetres above the floor so that the result was a more floating and ethereal space. (Foster 2011, 122).

Jan-Erik Andersson and Shawn Decker: *Bird's Nest Evanston*, Evanston Art Center, 2007.

Living in a nest

A journalist who visited our house whispered in my ear: "This is like living in a nest." She was not the first one to associate the house with a bird's nest. This was not an association Pitkäranta and I had in mind, but rather a bonus resulting from the floor plan's round shape, which is both cosy and energy-efficient. There is less wall surface in relation to the space to be heated than in a box-shaped house. This means that less energy is lost through wall surfaces.

This idea of living in a nest can be expanded to cover the *Bird's Nest* sculpture installations with their own soundscapes that I have built with the sound artist Shawn Decker.

I have employed a module made of lath triangles and built the nest using the same method a bird would, by joining a triangle to another according to a plan I have in my head and without using a tape measure. The outcome is a chaotic yet sturdy construction. It is built of triangular modules, but in a manner that makes it hard to see what a single set of modules looks like. Unlike those architects who have applied modules based on proportions of the human body to create repetitious and "people-friendly" architecture, I have used my module to create organised chaos.

Jonni Roos analyses the *Life on a Leaf* house with the view of the *Bird's Nest* installations in the Finnish Association of Architecture's publication *Arkkitehti* (3/2010).

The construction's chaotic impression derives from the use of one of the most disciplined forms. The works are ironic references to the module systems so dearly regarded by some architects, as well as animals' nest-building techniques. From the standpoint of architecture, the nests cobbled together by Andersson raise some serious questions. If nesting is a genetic need in other animals, why not in human beings? Should architecture – in order to meet needs that are species-typical for human beings – follow design principles that are compatible with these needs?

To live or not to live – in one's own head

About a century ago, Art Nouveau architects were accused of building houses that were too unique and therefore too difficult to subsequently sell. Now we can see that this criticism was misplaced, since in Finland Art Nouveau apartments are much sought after. Yet we hear the same arguments about the *Life on a Leaf* house; many people wonder how we dared to build a house so unique that hardly anyone else will want to live in it.

Of course, I asked myself this very question when we started designing the house. Our perspective, though, was not someone else's potential desire to buy the house. My problem was that I do not want to live in "my own head", i.e. in a house with aesthetics entirely based on my views. I think we managed to avoid this due to two reasons. One was my integrated collaboration with the architect Erkki Pitkäranta. We were equal in designing the architecture, which did not turn out to be a compromise, but a creative surprise for both of us. The other was the fact that we invited twenty artists to produce artwork for the house. The solutions may not strike you as particularly original, but in both cases I have taken the process a step further than what is usually done.

My collaboration with Pitkäranta has evolved during 15 years. Our method is to play, write stories, encourage one another to create new images that merge and then re-emerge as new, astounding images. In this case, the images were not only actual images painted or produced in other media, but inner and mental images. Gaston Bachelard describes imagination as a process that is beyond merely joining and working ready-made images. When the subconscious works, "new" images may merge.

If there is not a changing of images, an unexpected union of images, there is no imagination, no imaginative action. If a present image doesn't recall an absent one, if an occasional image does not give rise to a swarm of aberrant images, to an explosion of images, there is no imagination. (Bachelard 1979, 19).

Integrated collaboration has proven to be an excellent vehicle for reaching this innovative level, and it applies to the *Life on a Leaf* house, too. The process was initiated by an idea that Erkki threw into air: "Why not build a house of your own, say, in the shape of a leaf? You have used the leaf in many projects and sculptures before." I take it from there by making a cardboard model, a leaf as my starting point, and design a bluebell for the rooftop. I draw windows of various shapes. At one point Erkki bends the walls outward and removes the turret. I replace it with a Brazilian ferry that collides with the bluebell. The ferry becomes my computer studio. Erkki works on the ferry so that seen from above it looks like a huge tongue. The resemblance to the original ferry is really limited to the blue window frames and its oval shape. I add ornamentation to the exterior walls. This is really only an example. Our previous house projects have come to life through similar processes that share many features with the way Surrealists produced art.

We invited a group of artists, many from overseas and family friends, to break up my and Pitkäranta's aesthetics with a series of artworks that are integrated into the house's architecture. They were given free rein to come up with suggestions. I even encouraged them not to adapt their art to the architecture to ensure that the output would be surprising. This is how art and ornamentation should function in architecture: not to be amalgamated in it, but to provide contrast and comment, to revive architecture.

A house as an active organism

The feeling came very naturally during the construction process: this house is not a single-family house, but something else. It has a communicative dimension that operates on many levels.

I am not referring to inviting artists to join in the process or receiving groups of visitors and having attracted media attention. All this has given us an opportunity to meet people we would not have met otherwise.

No, there is something about the house, its architecture, interior and ornamentation that make it hard to describe it as "a single-family house". One reason is the fact that it is not easily associated with any existing house, particularly not with any standard single-family house. This applies to the house itself, the form of its windows and walls, as well as the appearance of its decor and ornamentation. The house refers to itself, to nature and also a fairyland through iconic forms (such as the leaf and bluebell), and to a variety of other phenomena through the artwork included in its architecture. This makes spending time in the house so fantastic. Since the house has neither a psychological nor a visual connection, through rectangular building masses, to the normal building tradition, it easily gives you the feeling of being on a "journey" where you are constantly acquiring new experiences. Although the house has now, after three years, become "normal", it still manages to give us the feeling of being somewhere else. There is always a new corner or a new glimmer of light that amazes you as you ponder all details and three-dimensional images (originating from iconic forms interacting with the surrounding world), which changes and is renewed when you walk around in the house. The feeling that you do not live in an ordinary house, in a system of boxes like many others do, but that you live in a unique "shell" of an organic form is tangible and liberating. This is enforced by the house's functionality on practical level. I only realise now how the box shape affects the ambiance of a home; with so few alternatives, we do not even consider this.

Another equally important reason is that we have left part of the ground floor as a public space. We deliberately keep as few personal items as possible there; only works of art by the other artists and few pieces by the family members. Yet this does not stop Adrian's toys from wandering downstairs from his room. We have, indeed, often thought that we live in a castle, not in a hermetically sealed modern royal house, but rather in the Versailles of Marie Antoinette's day. Then, the castle was public space where as many as 10,000 people could be found every day (Lever 2006, 30).

The living room – an opening six metres high over the green/white/black ornamented concrete floor – is a space that invites you to join in the dance. Especially on dark winter evenings the light entering indirectly from beneath the diagonal ceiling beams creates an ambience of a ball. It is very fitting that the floor ornamentation was inspired the story about Karin Månsdotter, who was the queen of Sweden for a short period of time. Our son Adrian loves having a disco on the floor, and guests, strangers to us before their visit, have jumped up to dance on it after a couple of glasses of wine.

It has also been interesting to have had semi-official visitors, artist colleagues, for instance, that I do not know very well. These meetings are special as our guests do not come just to see us, but primarily to see the house. Thus, the house has a special place in our lives. Thanks to all these associations with objects, organisms and phenomena that fill the house, the house has a particular way of linking an individual to the environment, and, of course, to the fairy tales and stories that the individual carries in his or her memory. In this case, the architecture is not a setting for a person's life or a machine for living in (the principal premises of contemporary architecture), but a kind of organism that creates its own life by influencing both us living here and our guests, and, through its exterior, even passers-by.

I think it would be good to point out here that obviously there is no direct link between the building and its inhabitants' happiness. You can live in your dream home and still be unhappy, or in a grey concrete apartment house and

be happy; it is an undeniable fact though, that houses and apartments create energy that has an effect on us. A fact that we should consider and research seriously.

Why are there not more leaf houses?

The written history of Western architecture has mainly associated it with the rational side of human behaviour. The shortest distance between two points is a straight line, and this is usually also the easiest to execute in terms of technology and energy. From this view point, it is natural that man's shelter against nature has been founded on simple geometric forms.

History, however, also shows that where enough time and money has been amassed, man has started to decorate his surroundings. This partly belongs to the irrational side of human behaviour, the side to which we should pay special attention. If beauty is channelled there with a caring small-scale approach, humour and imagination, it might help society head towards a better future.

Art and ornamentation were – until the breakthrough of Modernism – an element that was more or less detached from, yet a natural part of, architecture. Thus, buildings turned into total works of art. During the Modernist era, an idea of each art form's absolute independence was developed, whereby it would be possible to distil each art form's "essence". Art was then related to architecture in the form of replaceable paintings and/or sculptures.

Before Modernism we could enjoy façades and fixed décor that told their stories. The rich could afford to hire skilled artisans and artists, whereas others could build their individual houses and interiors aided by their creativity and handicraft skills.

Despite a surge in expressive and individual design during the past few decades, most architecture still follows the principles of minimalism. It emphasises concepts such as stylishness and functionality, and a more narrative, surprising and ornamental approach is seen as a manifestation of "bad taste". Eco-friendliness has also become part of minimalist building philosophy.

At least in Finland it appears there is no difference between industrial warehouses and grey, clean-surfaced

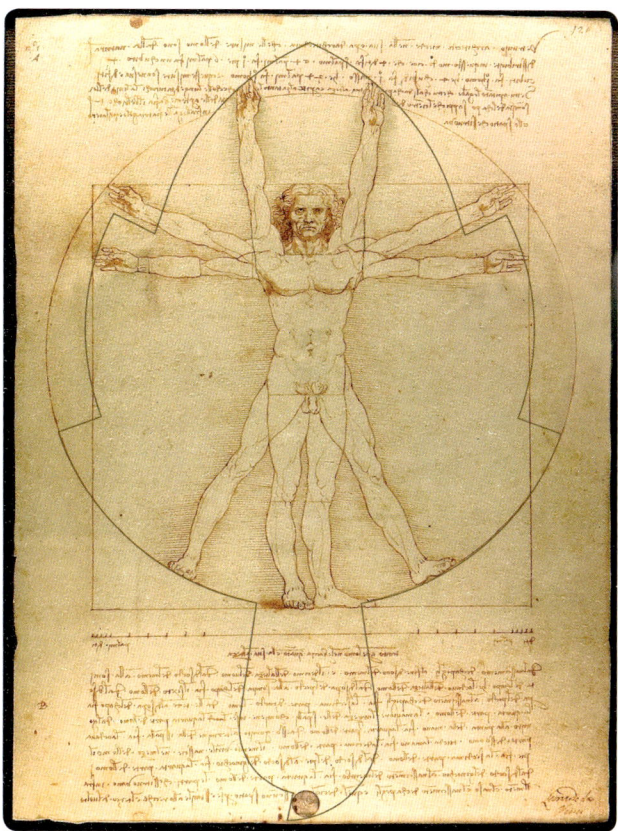

Jan-Erik Andersson: *Life on a Leaf and the Vitruvian Man*, 2010.

private houses designed by architects. I can understand why so many people decide to order prefabricated houses with ornamented window sills and Greek columns beside the main entrance. In our natural state, we are impressed by rich, stimulating and narrative environments. Architectural education nowadays teaches a philosophy that is too restricted in its focus on the superiority of simplification and the abstract, which we need to be taught to appreciate in order to enable the humankind to develop.

And what do artists do? Dismissed, voluntarily or otherwise, from their original role in participating in the creation of total works of art and public spaces (we should keep in mind that many works of art, now displayed in art museums, were made for a particular space), they seem to enjoy the new marginal, yet perhaps more independent role, and content themselves with operating in temporary environments of galleries, museums and townscapes. The German critic and writer Gerrith Gohlke, in his lecture in a seminar on the relationship of art and architecture at the Finnish Academy of Fine Arts, said that artists should steer clear of architecture.

But if we take another approach and ask whether there are architects who are keen on in-depth collaboration with artists, we can find several interesting examples, the most famous of which may be Frank Gehry's collaboration with Claes Oldenburg. The RIBA-awarded architect Will Alsop is always on the lookout for new means of producing architecture, and demands that artists become more involved: "The role of the artist in determining our external experience is essential. Without the artist, the role falls to the landscape architects and/or the urban designers. Current art practice goes way beyond the idea of the object placed in space" (Alsop 2004, 25).

Many architects are burdened with tight budgets and deadlines. Developers usually require that houses be built as cost-effectively as possible, and this often results in getting rid of anything extra, which includes art and ornamentation. The house projects I have carried out with Erkki Pitkäranta have proven, though, that creating livelier architecture does not need to be a financial issue. The problem lies, rather, in the current aesthetic taste in Finland that favours minimalist, mainly grey, surfaces.

The *Life on a Leaf* house, by its existence, shows that a large part of the philosophy generated by architectural theory over the centuries does not concern itself with the creation of stimulating environments. Rather, it is an abstract and rational philosophical construction that has helped to fossilise an idea of architecture as buildings based on the square and the circle equipped with a varying amount of artistic ornamentation. *The Vitruvian Man*, designed in 1487 by Leonardo da Vinci, is inscribed in a square and circle; it is used as a proof that architecture based on geometric basic forms is connected to the human body (as well as to the human mind). In the drawing beside, I have placed the *Life on a Leaf* floor plan around the Vitruvian Man by only raising his arms a little! Geometry and mathematics are essential tools in construction, but leaving a house's "soul" in their hands would be a mistake.

Human or not, rational architecture surely originated in simple structures that could be built without high-tech tools. According to the Abbot Laugier (1713–69), all architecture relies on a kind of standard, a primitive hut made of vertical trunks or perhaps of growing trees, on top of which horizontal narrow trunks are placed and then smaller trunks crosswise on top of these. This standard was the model for Greek columns, foundations, architraves and ornaments (twigs and leaves left on trunks), and it is not far removed from buildings that were the basis of Vitruvius's view of what architecture should look like or from the theory according to which the only relevant shapes for a floor plan are the square and circle, and, derived from these, the rectangle and the oval.

I find it suspicious that over 2,000 years later the main body of all architectural theory leads back to Vitruvius's book *De Architectura* (1st century BC) – one single book! Technology is so advanced now that we can design buildings of any shape we want. It is time we redefined the concept of architecture; it is no longer possible that the profession could theoretically exclude from its framework constructions whose foundations lie on other concepts such as figurative forms.

It is bizarre how the Vitruvian Man has managed to wander, theoretically unchallenged, through the halls of architectural teaching for centuries. In France, Claude-Nicolas Ledoux (1736–1806) came up with some interesting models for figurative architecture, architechture parlante, none of which were realised unfortunately. In the Baroque and Art Nouveau periods, a number of environments based on irrational and natural elements and forms were built, but it says a lot that very few of these were supported by any theories, whereas rational architects produced texts in profusion. It is these texts that give them status. More expressive architecture is easier to understand and does not require great intellectual support, but it is easily defeated by overwhelming "rational" arguments. We have a good example in Finland. The *Canon 60* system by the architect Aulis Blomstedt (1906–79) was an attempt at harmonious box architecture that was supported by an incredible number of mathematical formulas. In the early 20th century, even the fine arts tried to build a universal system for beauty. For example, Wassily Kandinsky examined the essence of the point and line in his book *Punkt und Linie zu Fläche* (1926), but did not – luckily – manage to develop a prescriptive system for art-making.

At the end of the 18th century, even Vitruvius was accused of over-emphasising a building's aesthetic features. He was, after all, particular in his opinion that a building should include ornamentation, but this should not be exaggerated. For example, he was appalled by terrible illusionist paintings that did not observe the laws of gravity. Yet Vitruvius did not want architects to apply ornamentation merely for the sake of it; rather, what it expressed had to be taken into consideration. He observed that caryatides (female figures) were used instead of columns because they symbolised the event when the Greeks quashed a rebellion in the town of Karyes, killing the men and condemning the women to slavery. This is how their punishment might be handed down even to posterity. There must be a clear underlying idea (Vitruvius 2009, 1.1.5).

A turning point in the relationship between artistic elements and rationality came in France at the end of the 18th century, when the training of architects was transferred from the artistic École des Beaux-Arts to the École Polytechnique. This manifested itself in architects such as Jean-Nicolas-Louis Durand (1760–1834), who laid the bases for hard-core Modernism by distancing themselves from the Vitruvian tradition and from the idea that architecture should hold a mathematic and mimetic relation to the human body. For Durand, architecture and town planning were concerned with the square and the right angle (Kruft 1994, 273–74). It is telling that Durand adopted the metric system that had been implemented in France in 1795 instead of using the old anthropometric system based on foot and inch.

Even Modernism was not quite as pure and clear as it would like us to believe. In this context, Le Corbusier is an interesting point of study as his production includes a great deal of irrationality and contradiction.

If the premises for defining architecture are solely a geometric plan, walls and light, as is the case with Le Corbusier and numerous others, the outcome is what we now see in many places: impersonal and nondescript architecture.

But architecture does not consist of only those features that Le Corbusier's manifesto addresses. Paradoxically, this was proven by Le Corbusier himself in many of his buildings that I mention in the Theory Book. It is just the beginning! For a building to be "complete", it needs ornamentation that "provides" it to people. This can be achieved through two methods: either by covering the entire exterior and interior with ornamentation or by giving the building a sculptural form so it becomes an ornament in itself. This is typical of so-called iconic buildings ("Wow" architecture) that have been built over the past ten years.

They demonstrate a revived interest in ornamentation, and not only in décor, but also in the exterior appearance, the part of a building that communicates with its surroundings. A building is no longer just a machine for living in, but also a visual element in our environment, and hence an inspiration for the spiritual environment where we live and meet others.

Some views are more critical. Hal Foster, in *The Art-Architecture complex*, misses the original Modernism, which, in his opinion, was characterised by literal transparency and where glass was glass and steel was steel (Foster 2011, 124–). Foster thinks that contemporary architecture is marked by fragmental and grotesque transparency where various projections (from printed images and patterns, light installations, half-transparent plastic panels etc.) are attached to a building's "skin". An example he mentions is the Blur Building by Diller Scofidio + Renfro, built for the Swiss Expo 2002. The building is surrounded by a cloud of mist that is produced in the foundation using water from Lake Neuchâtel below. There is a bar on the top level where they serve spring water from all over the world as well as water from thawing glaciers.

To underline the building's virtual quality, visitors can create a digital profile for themselves and are given devices that react when they bump into another person with similar profile. The communion of architecture, design and art is total, since Diller Scofidio + Renfro also display a video installation of the *Blur Building* in museums; it was shown for example at the WILD exhibition I curated at the Turku City Art Museum (WAM) in 2007.

Foster talks to Richard Serra, who, for him, is a proponent of original, pure and clear Modernist thinking. Serra's enormous sheet metal sculptures deal with tectonic problems such as balance and the weight of the structure; all the joints and fitting systems are visible. You can see links

to the round shapes that were present in the early days of Modernist architecture.

But however much you appreciate the spaciousness that comes with clean masses, I insist that it is ornamental elements that enliven a space. It is regrettable that many architecture commentators refuse to approach architecture from the ornamental angle.

The *Life on a Leaf* house demonstrates how different it is to live in a house that is aimed at creating "iconic space" from living in an abstract cube. For many, I suspect, this is a very marginal problem, and some may view it the same way as the visitor who, astounded, asked me why I went on about nature. "You only need to step outside and it's there!" Which, of course, is true; at least in Finland. The comment implies that you can live in a box-shaped house; the house itself needs not represent nature. If we want to feel connected to nature, the quickest and most sensible way to achieve this is to go out and enjoy nature as it is.

However, for many people, their relationship with nature is not so unambiguous, and they prefer to stay in an urban setting. Our family does not have a summer home or a boat. To me, art is an essential part of urban "nature". The relationship between nature and culture may not be quite as polarised as it used to be. Very little of original forests remain. Most of the land considered as nature in Europe has been touched by the human hand. Nature has no use for art, but a person torn away from a direct and comprehensive, often sublime experience of nature seems to crave a way to fill the void. For many, art becomes a positive, feel-good substitute. This gradual transition from nature to culture is fascinating, and biotechnology will make it even more so in future.

The *Life on a Leaf* house will settle somewhere in this area, as a means to gradually transfer the surrounding nature to the mental space in the human mind. Based on my experience of living in the house, I think it would be good for people – whose genetic makeup is designed to work in nature – to live in an environment based on natural forms. It has been important for me to test what it feels like to exclude the square from the house's structure, the ultimate symbol of the notion that "we are not part of nature".

In a densely-built urban environment with very few trees and other vegetation, architecture that takes its inspiration from natural forms is a kind of substitute nature. It contributes, together with ample vegetation, to enlivening an urban environment, making it friendlier than "cold" Modernism could – and late Modernism can.

Even though I do not disagree with building cubes – just as any type of building, they can be designed well and not so well – I see basic geometric forms more as a foundation on which to build complex, figurative and ornamental systems.

Where are we?

Anthony Vidler describes the early 21st century as a period when the definition of space will change. Artists become interested in architectural elements in their installation work, which in a way is criticism of traditional art forms. At the same time, architects are studying artists' processes to rid themselves of the strict codes on Functionalism and Formalism.

This intersection has engendered a kind of "intermediary art", comprised of objects that, while situated osemsibly in one practice, require the interpretive terms of another for their explication. (Widler 2000, viii).

One approach to the *Life on a Leaf* house is to consider it as a *Gesamtkunstwerk*, a total work of art. Professor George H. Marcus of the University of Pennsylvania visited the house in order to examine its role within this tradition. He said it differed from other total works of art in that the invited artists were given free rein to create surprises. The outcome is not controlled in the same way as total works of art tend to be.

This element of surprise, and the fact that the house was inspired by stories written as free-flowing fantasies aimed at reaching the subconscious, have made a link to a search for a surrealistic house of dreams and memories (*oneiric house*).

The traditional Surrealists, however, did not manage to produce houses under their philosophy, with the exception of Salvador Dalí's *Dream of Venus Pavilion* at the 1939 New York World's Fair. Although André Breton liked Gaudí's expressive buildings and DYI projects such as Facteur Cheval's *Palais Idéal* (1879–1912), Tristan Tzara lived in a disciplined house designed by Adolf Loos. Thus it is not surprising that facets of Surrealism have been sought in Modernism. Concepts such as "sublime architecture", i.e. the idea that architecture does not have to be beautiful, but that it may stir effusive emotions by being brutal, monotonous and grand, can be applied to link these types of buildings to the notion of "the architectural uncanny" coined by Anthony Vidler. These unpleasant and repressed emotions were of interest to Surrealists too. Thomas Mical's anthology *Surrealism and Architecture* has a picture of a Le Corbusier house on its cover and many of its articles highlight Surrealist elements in Le Corbusier's architecture, despite the fact that Breton was an adversary of Modernist architecture.

Even Dalibor Vesely shows his disapproval in his essay *The Surreal House*:

The apparent proximity of Le Corbusier's approach and surrealism reveals nevertheless a fundamental difference – that between creativity based on explicit, conscious use of analogies and creativity based on dream-inspired oneiric analogies that "reveal the deep relation between

distant realities which the logical functioning of our mind cannot link together". It is for this reason that works such as the Beistegui apartment (Le Corbusier) or the projects of Coop Himmelb(l)au cannot be described as true surrealist architecture, but only as architecture that came to existence under the influence or in the shadow of surrealism. (Vesely 2010, 41).

It is amazing that there are countless dream-like building projects all over the world, many by DYI builders, which could be labelled as surrealistic, yet very few of these are featured in books on Surrealist architecture. Surrealism is viewed through the critical filter of Modernism and even Dalí's theatre-museum in Figueres is usually left out. It is particularly regrettable because Surrealist architecture is defined by Hal Foster, as quoted in Jane Alison's *The Surreal House*, as the opposite of Modernism:

(Hal) Foster describes the surrealist house as "a hysterical body", characterized, as he says, by the ornamental and outmoded, a house that is irrevocably associated with the feminine, the infantile and the historical. Modernism, by contrast, attempted to iron out all the folds, pretend there were no in-between-spaces, no dirt, no dust, no old furniture – no desire. (Alison 2010, 22).

It is exactly these notions that Foster uses to describe Surrealist architecture that could be applied to the *Life on a Leaf* house. Even the other terms we have used to describe our house come close to the Surrealist theory: stories, play, roundness, poetry, memories, embraceability, fairy tales, nature, Art Nouveau, surprise, ruins, opposites, recycled items, extraversion, introversion, ornamentation, window, dream.

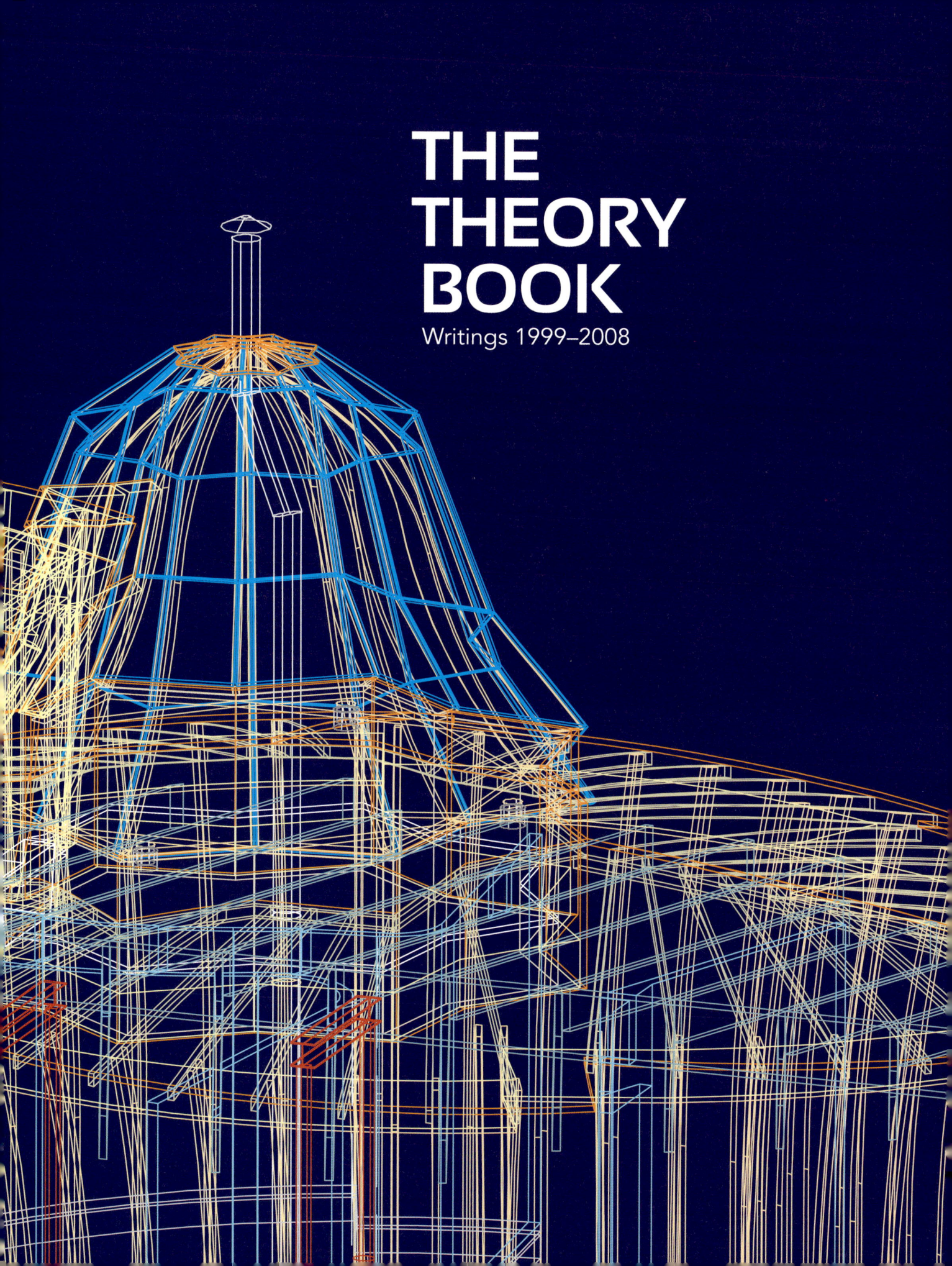

The author plays with an F1 slot car track. The garbage bin mentioned in the text is in the right upper corner of the picture. Turku, 1966.

Ornate antennae. Photo taken in Istanbul 2005.

The inner room

I remember how my brother and I used to lie in our beds in our little room when we were children, looking at the ceiling where the lights from passing cars shone in, forming ever-changing designs that looked like tiny openings into eternity. Combined with the buzzing from the engines, they sent me into a half-conscious sleep.

In the daytime the floor of our room turned into a town where we encountered exciting adventures and raced around on our F1 slot car track. Sometimes we pushed the waste paper bin into the corner between the bookcase and wall, suddenly turning the room into the size of a basketball court.

When we attempt to define a space, it is difficult to distinguish the external, physical space from the internal space created in our consciousness. It seems simple, on the surface. We use stone, timber, concrete, clay, steel and glass to build a house or a shelter to protect us from the elements. We can knock on the wall and it is like any other physical object. But as soon as we step or crawl inside – and light the fire, perhaps, to warm ourselves up – once we feel safe, there is a change. Even if the shelter is just a cardboard den, small and wobbly, it gives us an intimate experience of the space, which then allows us to use our imagination.

The philosopher Gaston Bachelard writes in *The Poetics of Space*: "the house is one of the greatest powers of integration for the thoughts, memories and dreams of mankind. The binding principle in this integration is the daydream." (Bachelard 1994, 6.)

> "Thinking is the best way to travel."
>
> Moody Blues, 1968

As we grow up, we should not give up on imagination. A window in a small flat may open up the feeling of space until it embraces an entire world. That is why it is so important to be able to see the sky and the horizon when living in a confined space, the way I am, even now, writing this article. I lie on a couch, intentionally bought for the purpose of daydreaming, beside the window and watch clouds go by. In no time I'm on a plane and soon in a rocket on my way into the cold iciness of space.

For those who live in cramped spaces, the four walls of their homes are increasingly gaining openings. The latest expansion of mental space comes via the internet. I remember how excited I was when the internet was first introduced and I was able to just click and be whisked away to different continents, or to send a message anywhere on the planet in just a second. We can now use voice and video chat to expand our living rooms and reach our friends who are thousands of miles away.

Margaret Wertheim considers how virtual media will change our materialistic world view:

> *It is just the mind, the heart, the soul – in short the human psyche – that has been banished from the picture of reality that Western physics has articulated over the past three hundred years […] in the potentially infinite web of the internet, the "soul" has once again found a space that it might call its own (Wertheim 1998, 48).*

Even though faith in information technology has subsided to a more sensible level since Wertheim wrote the above in the 1990^s, it is quite clear that digital communication and image saving techniques will expand our sense of space both backwards and forwards. I have been taking digital pictures of my son, who was born in 2004, nearly every day. When he is a grown-up man, he will be able to return to his early years and may be able to better understand himself as a person by observing the environments and people that surrounded him in his formative years. I hope the pictures I have taken are so good and ambiguous that they will not deprive him of his "magic memories".

The virtual world changes our relationship with the surrounding reality in many ways. I am not really referring to the mental world expanded by voice and video chat nor the significance of computer programmes in the architecture of organic forms, rather I think that virtual reality will set us free from the concept of Zeitgeist, from the idea that architecture progresses in a linear manner and that a new style is required to manifest the zeitgeist.

Thanks to laptops and wireless internet connections, we can keep in touch with the present regardless of where we are, whether in the countryside, among ruins of Ancient Rome, in a Renaissance palace, a dramatic Baroque church, an organic Art Nouveau villa or Elsa Beskow's fairy tale *The Children of Hat Cottage*. We are in the centre of a polygonal sphere, where the vectors point in every direction. We can define our reality whichever way we like and we can detach ourselves from all stylistic constraints.

In the virtual – and visual – world of the 21st century, it is easy to forget, however, that the most effective medium of daydreams and imagination is still the written text. In the still of the night, lying in a comfortable bed in an intimate room, we can read and let fictional worlds mould our minds.

Childhood memories shape our later existence. I have been subconsciously attracted to houses similar to those where I lived when I was young, built in the 1950^s, before the emergence of prefabricated houses. Despite their outward greyness, they were well-designed and often placed in park-like and varied surroundings and adapted to the site. Even if these buildings do not feature traditional ornamentation, there is an abundance of memorable details, such as wooden banisters.

Budapest, Aulich utca 3. Photo taken in 2011.

Elsa Beskow: Illustration for the story *Branden i Fäderköping*, 1932.

Elsa Beskow: Illustration for the story *The Children of Hat Cottage*, 1930

It is no coincidence, surely, that while we are waiting for the *Life on a Leaf* house to be finished, my family and I are staying in a one bedroom apartment built in that era. The building is situated about a hundred metres from the hospital where I was born, in the same neighbourhood where I was pushed around in my pram. In today's rootless world, it is a luxury to be able to live in the environment that shaped me; one that still holds so many memories and meanings for me.

My childhood mindscape was strongly influenced by the fairy tales I heard and later read myself. I believe that stories can create particular moods in our minds, spaces to which we can later return to in order to seek shelter and safety. In my opinion, the moods and sentiments created by our imaginations, memories and stories are vital to our mental health.

My thesis and the basis for this research is the idea that these mental spaces need a surface where they can be reflected within our living environments, so that they can be activated and retrieved. To achieve this, it is important that the architecture surrounding us stimulates us with means of form, ornamentation and spatial structure, as well as the art that is part of the architecture. I maintain that only a small portion of present-day architecture works this way, unfortunately. For the *Life on a Leaf* house project, I am collaborating with the architect Erkki Pitkäranta, and our aim is to find a way to create such an environment.

Of all the writers whose work I heard and read as a child, I would like to mention three who were particularly important to me: Tove Jansson, Astrid Lindgren and Elsa Beskow. The moods present in their books feature in many of my installations, sculptures and public artworks that have been produced since the early 1980^s, as well as in the buildings I have created with Erkki Pitkäranta since 1995. I also feel an affinity with the way they combine text with illustration.

Therefore, it is not surprising that many critics place my art in the same category as with artists who take their themes from their memories.

> *Homemade fairy tales lie behind the figurative installations of Jan-Erik Andersson. His works are usually about love, longing and nostalgia. The intention is to create sculptures and installations that inspire children and adults to create their own fantasies and stories, and to this end he uses bright colours, simple shapes and cartoon-like figures (Collins 2007, 286).*

I'd like to refer to Collins' words "inspire children and adults". I do not think that it is merely a question of nostalgia and longing for childhood, but rather a heartfelt notion that the mood so typical of these writers is universal, and that it should play an important role in the "grown-up" world too.

I chose a story by Elsa Beskow as the basis for the theoretical part of my research. In her book *Landet Långthärifrån* (*The Land of Long Ago*), there is a story called *Branden i Fläderköping*. In the beginning of the story, the entire town of Fläderköping is destroyed by fire. A rich man, who lived in the town as a child, walks by and promises to help the townspeople. He has one condition, though: the houses must be built so that it is clear who lives in each house. (Beskow 1932). The illustrations depict fantastical houses that could be in a textbook for architects that I would love to write myself.

In another book by Beskow, *Hattstugan* (*The Children of Hat Cottage*), the reader is invited to fill in the missing words with ones that rhyme. Two children and their mother look at their cottage, which is made out of a hat. The text goes:

En lustig stuga hade de fått fatt.
De bodde i en gammal kvarglömd _

Men barnen tyckte att de bodde flott.
De tyckte hatten var ett riktigt _

The missing words are "hatt" and "slott" ("hat" and "castle"). What is interesting is the two opposing attitudes. "Grown-ups" are expected to see the cottage as an old hat, while children can see a fabulous castle.

The English translation[1] doesn't follow the Swedish word by word, so this conflict is only perceived in the original Swedish version.

I see some questions in this conflict of ideas that I hope to be able to clarify. Why is the children's world and the adults' world so strongly opposed to each other? Why is it childish to live in a unique colourful house that looks like an object? Why is there not a single house that is shaped like a hat, flower or shoe among the millions of box-shaped houses? Why is contemporary Finnish architecture so strongly characterized by minimalism?

How do visual arts influence architecture? By building the *Life on a Leaf* house I wanted to study if the use of figurative shapes, mostly taken from nature, in the design of the house (floorplan, shapes of the windows, ornamentation etc.) would create a different sense of space in the consciousness of the inhabitant than the Modernist space created mostly by cleaan walls, light and rectangular shapes. Some comments on these issues, based on living in the finished house, can be found in chapter *Afterword*.

Today's "solemn" adults seem to think that play belongs to leisure time, to the beach and parties. Playfulness appears to be an almost impossible feature in contemporary architecture – in Finland as well as everywhere else – if one wants to be taken seriously as an architect. Often, the reason given for the idea that architecture should be "serious" and minimalist is financial circumstances. In this book, I want to claim that aesthetic choices play an equally big role. They steer architecture towards a direction where ornamentation is often replaced, in a sophisticated manner, by abstract details and surface structures that refer to nothing else but themselves and technology.

Even though I now live near my roots again, I have lived in buildings representing different architectural styles and this has made me realise that they each had a different influence on me. There is really only one style that makes me feel completely at home and truly feeds my imagination: Art Nouveau. For this reason, it seems natural to start my thesis by explaining how Art Nouveau differs from other construction designs.

Gesellius, Lindgren & Saarinen: Fabianinkatu 17, next to Kasarmintori. Helsinki, 1901.

[1] *The little woman and her three children lived in a little cottage. It was the shape of a hat! They called it Hat Cottage.*

The children loved their little cottage and their mother kept it as clean as a king's castle.

English version © Floris Books 2012

Art Nouveau – Living as an adventure

"Form follows fun."
Origin unknown

There have been times when daydreaming and imagination have momentarily been allowed in architecture. A period that was interesting in this respect was the short yet influential era of the Art Nouveau movement, which lasted for a couple of decades from 1890 until around 1910.

The term Art Nouveau is used to describe an architectural movement that wanted to free itself from a strictly classicistic idiom to find authentic individual expression. Belgian Art Nouveau architect Victor Horta (1861–1947) said that traditional and familiar elements disappeared in his new architectural works, to be replaced by elements that emerged from his own mind (Loze 1991, 22).

Late 19th century architecture was characterised by eclecticism, which combined and reused historical styles in various ways. There was a frantic search for a new, uniform style. The answer was Art Nouveau, a combination of new iron and glass technologies with attention given to handicraft, organic forms and regional traditions.

The term Art Nouveau was used in Belgium and France, the two pioneering countries of the style. I will apply the term to the entire movement, which was known in various countries by various names. In Austria, Germany and Finland it was known as *Jugendstil or Jugend*, in Spain as *Modernisme* and in Russia as *Stil Modern*.

Art Nouveau took advantage of developing industries that made it possible to build light structures using iron and glass, yet it was also a reaction to industrialisation with its inhuman practices. Before World War I, there were still craftsmen and cheap labour available so buildings could be embellished with a great deal of ornamentation.

Bold, innovative use of different materials was characteristic of the style; for instance, cast iron was combined with ceramic tiles and glass. The history of local architecture became a point of interest. In Finland, for example, medieval stone churches became an inspiration. The objective was to create impressive total works of art, which viewers find interesting even today. Art Nouveau wanted to prove that the hierarchy according to which art forms were categorised and which stated that handicrafts had no value was no longer relevant. Many architects who were active in the movement worked with different art forms; Henry Van de Velde, for example, began as a painter. No element was considered insignificant in Art Nouveau; rather it was believed that all elements worked together when turning living into an adventure.

Practitioners of Finnish Art Nouveau, or *Jugendstil*, produced very unique, unpolished and simplistic architecture. Here too, the first ornamentation of the period was unrestrained and inspired by Finnish mythology, though the idiom later became more abstract and controlled. Marika Hausen describes how the transition period affected *Hvitträsk* (Kirkkonummi, Finland), the total work of art completed in 1903 designed by Gesellius, Lindgren and Saarinen: "The decoration in *Hvitträsk* was quite subtle and there were no goblins to be seen" (Hausen 2000, 24).

I do not understand why they had to leave the goblins out, since the residential building the trio designed in Helsinki, at Fabianinkatu 17, is beautiful and inspiring with its frog and goblin decorated façade. The building is also a great example of the Art Nouveau principle of constructing houses from the inside out, i.e. starting with the inhabitants' needs and designing the

Hector Guimard: *Castle Béranger*, 14 Rue La Fontaine, Paris, 1890.

Architecture as art: apartment building in Paris signed by Hector Guimard in 1911.

space accordingly. The exterior is then formed as a result of the interior plan. (Moorhouse 1998, 33.) The apartments were designed to be cosy homes with interesting details and juxtaposing materials, resulting in a building with an asymmetrical exterior that changes its shape when viewed from various angles. Another fine example is Hector Guimard's apartment building, *Castel Béranger* (1890), at 14 Rue La Fontaine, Paris. The Modernist approach to construction was often the exact opposite: a building was expected above all to appear as an aesthetic whole when seen from the outside.

Hvitträsk is also a proof of what seamless integrated cooperation can mean. "It was built at a time when the three architect friends collaborated very closely and fruitfully; it is often impossible to tell who designed what in the office" (Hausen 2000, 30–32).

Art Nouveau's influence was, however, short-lived. After World War I there was a need for an architectural movement that advocated a new and better future. Modernism, with its ideas of clean, simplistic and industrially produced forms, was the obvious answer. Art Nouveau was seen as an unproductive and incoherent chapter in the history of architecture. Its greatest works, such as buildings designed by Frank Lloyd Wright, Josef Hoffman, Charles Rennie Mackintosh and Louis Sullivan, were thought to contain hidden geometry and clean surfaces considered as heralds of Modernism.

In my opinion, this claim is history written by the victors, underrating the holistic view and love of ornamentation, intimacy and detail expressed by these architects. An example of this is the slogan "form follows function", which became one of the fundamental principles of functionalism. It was coined by American architect Louis Sullivan (1856–1924), whose buildings show early signs of the emphasis on clean, ornament-free surfaces.

The phrase, however, has been taken out of context. It is often left unmentioned that Sullivan was a master of the decorated surface. He did say that architects should practise with "unadorned" masses for several years, but having mastered that, they should consider how to decorate buildings individually in order to give them their own character. According to Sullivan, a building should be unique in the same way that human beings are. This means that the ornamentation must even be considered during the planning phase, so that the building is an organic structure (Sullivan 1892, 284–287).

In practical terms, the victory of Modernism was almost complete, and several practitioners of Art Nouveau, e.g. Peter Behrens and also Victor Horta, to some extent, surrendered and adopted a more severe concept of architecture. Art Nouveau's taste for the original and the handmade did not quite meet the contemporary requirements of mass production.

Some of Art Nouveau's finest ideas actually contributed to its downfall. One was the objective of making buildings reflect their owners, acting as their portraits. This kind of communication with the client was particularly important to Horta (Loze 1991, 182). However, this approach was risky for many investors as any building that was too unique might be difficult to sell. We now know that this is not the case. In Finland, for instance, Art Nouveau apartments are in great demand.

Pierre Loze points to another reason for the decline: the less talented successors of the real masters, such as Horta, exaggerated features. This led to equally exaggerated opposition to the works created during this "decadent" period (Ibid., 152.) Even Horta's idiom became a little more restrained around 1901 after he designed *Hotel Aubecq* (1899), which was an adventure in a daydream. The building was demolished in 1950.

In this context, Loze mentions that the spontaneous nature so typical of Horte's oeuvre seems to disappear after 1898, when it was replaced by his

Louis Sullivan: Carson, Pirie, Scott and Company Building, Chicago, 1899.

Louis Sullivan: Bayard-Condict Building, 65–69 Bleecker Street, New York, 1897–99.

Victor Horta: *Hôtel Tassel*, Brussels, 1894. Wikimedia Commons.

Ornamentation on the roof/ceiling. Antoni Gaudí: *Casa Milà*, Barcelona, 1910.

Antoni Gaudí: *Casa Battló*, Barcelona, 1907.

perfect mastery of architecture. After committing himself to finding an architectural design that returned to its roots and was free from conventions, Horta again took up the cultural values that had brought about order and peace in the midst of chaos since Antiquity. This meant the return to classical values, to the accumulated experience of the architects who since the times of Greece and Rome had thought about the art of building houses, and also the return to modesty after an act of utmost courage, pride and inventiveness (Ibid., 152). To Horta, this also meant communicating with the masters who had taught him the basics of architecture. Yet this does not, by any means, imply that Horta wanted to "make a clear sweep" like Modernists did (Ibid., 199).

Loze also describes Horta's relationship with his buildings as a means for a shy and reclusive man to communicate with the outside world. To him, a building and its inhabitants were important, and the building served as a way to dialogue with the client. Unfortunately, Horta did not receive the recognition he so badly needed but was, instead, treated with derision by subsequent owners, who radically changed the buildings to get rid of the dated style. Many of his buildings were demolished.

Horta's aim to create innovative architecture without borrowing from elsewhere was a success, but he had many followers who wished to turn the expression into a style, which Horta did not like. He did not see his buildings as permanent, but instead thought that if people found them worth preserving, they could do so. He also thought that it might have been wiser to experiment with a more traditional architectural idiom– he would have escaped tasteless imitation and might have gained broader recognition (Ibid., 184).

Antoni Gaudí's buildings in Barcelona also attracted harsh criticism and mockery. His buildings were likened to cakes and they were said to have been designed to attract potential buyers just like any other articles for sale:

Seeing the way in which the 1900 architects had deformed the materials, making them lose all their tectonic qualities, their contemporaries used the metaphors of the patisserie for these buildings made of cake. This was true even by 1929 when Francis Carco wrote about La Pedrera and before which, in 1910, in a caricature by Junceda a small boy exclaimed Daddy, daddy, I want an Easter egg as big as this one...

This is definitely not referring to a soft, sweet or kind image like that of cakes. On the contrary, it is contemptuous and cruel, and derives from the intuition that the public, anonymous and wishful, had of the way in which architecture had become just as any other product on display on the marketplace (Lahuerta 2003, 41–42).

Gaudí is one of the architects who have had the most influence on me. The way he used the history of Catalonia, the local environment, new technology, ornamentation, art, imagination and even sound (he had holes drilled on the *Sagrada Familia's* towers to enable the wind to produce sounds) makes him a master of creating an "iconic space". But since Gaudí is so well-known, I have chosen to leave him out of the scope of this study. I do hope, though, that despite such a brief comment on Gaudí, my readers will understand how important an inspiration he has been to both this text and the *Life on a Leaf* house.

Lars Sonck: *The Story of the Mushrooms*, facade of the Mikaelinkirkko church, Turku, 1905

Gesellius, Lindgren & Saarinen: *Pohjolan talo*, Aleksanterinkatu 44, Helsinki. Sculptures/ornaments by Hilda Flodin, 1901.

Flóris Korb and Kálmán Giergl: Ferenc Liszt Music Academy, Budapest, 1907.

Jaques Rosenbaum: Pikk 18, Tallinna, 1910. Sculptures August Volz.

Lars Arrhenius: *Streetlife*. The pictogram windows penetrate through the walls into the living rooms and create iconic spaces.
Hammarby sea city, Mältaren quarter, Stockholm, 2010. Photo: Lars Arrhenius.

"Everyone knows and feels how strongly individual is each man's voice, but few pause to consider that a voice, though of another kind, speaks from every existing building. What is the character of these voices? Are they harsh or smooth, noble or ignoble? Is the speech they utter prose or poetry?"

Louis Sullivan, 1892

Life on a Leaf, Art Nouveau and Modernism

I find Art Nouveau and its philosophy appealing; to build a house as a shelter and a source of inspiration for man's inner world, as opposed to the Modernist view that "the house is a machine for living in" (Le Corbusier 1986, 95).

One reason why Art Nouveau was defeated by Modernism was the fact that the former style's preferred aesthetics were dependent on craftsmanship, thus making it much more expensive to produce than unembellished modernist surfaces free of traditional ornamentation.

But now, a hundred years later, new technologies allow us to use CAD software and computer-based cutting technology in designing buildings, details and ornaments. Although the technology is still quite expensive, we could ask ourselves whether we would like to revive more innovative architecture.

I think we have arrived at a very complex historical period, which, if we are talking about art and architecture, is hard to fit into definitions such as late Modernism or Postmodernism. For many, including myself, though, a belief in linear, ever-improving progress has been replaced by a view of history as a series of events. Each event is valuable as such, and we can revisit them to find information that is important to those of us who are living in the here and now.

In the *Life on a Leaf* project, architect Erkki Pitkäranta and I aim to find out whether it would be possible to apply Art Nouveau's ideas to a house built using present-day technology. To me this means that:

- the aesthetics of the house are guided by natural forms;
- the house's shape and details stimulate the imagination;
- we apply ornamentation inspired by nature and/or by representational elements from fairytales;
- the house is built as a total work of art, where artists and artisans are invited to produce works that are incorporated into the architecture;
- we contrast various forms, aesthetic ideas and materials in order to prevent the house from becoming an example of one single style;
- we introduce, through the project, various examples of how to create an" iconic space".

I would like to highlight another objective: to examine whether a house can be imbued with content, "a soul", by writing stories for it; stories that could be an inspiration for ornaments, décor and its external form. This would then preclude the creation of ornaments without meaning. Five of these stories,

Antoni Gaudí: *Casa Milà*, Barcelona, 1910. The railings of the balconies, designed by Josep Maria Jujol, aim to give an impression of seaweed washed up onto the shore. Gaudí's intention was that the residents would grow plants to enhance the visual effect.

Sculptures by August Volz on the facade of an apartment building in Tallinn, 1909.

written to influence the design of the *Life on a Leaf* house are printed in the *Afterwords* section of the book.

An oft-repeated argument against ornamentation is that we are no longer capable of producing it (Loos 1908, 289). During the *Life on a Leaf* project, I intend to study what contemporary ornamentation might look like.

I am going to prove that a building's "soul" is not in its abstract, plain frame, but in the ornamental and artistic details that are organically integrated into the architectural body and that make the building "stand out".

Unlike in Modernist aesthetics, art should not be a detachable element, such as a framed painting that can be changed, but rather an indivisible part of architecture.

When asked to describe why a particular building's architecture is art, many architects from the Modernist camp point to the harmony of the constructional elements and the way light plays on the façade and in the rooms. Architect and professor Kaj Nyman talks about "houses' language". In his letter to me says: "One only becomes an architect after learning the language following a long period of practice. It is more a question of the rooms' proportions, light, scale and materials than one of 'design'. […] When I try to visualise your house… I can't see any union of art and architecture. I'm sure it will be art but architecture?" (Nyman 17/8/2000).

According to this view, it is the abstract elements that constitute the core of the concept of architecture. This will easily lead to the idea that ornamentation and artistic works are unnecessary "garnishes". In my opinion, ornamentation plays an equally, perhaps even more important part in the creation of the mental spaces that are formed in our brains, where our thoughts and emotions reside.

But what was it that caused the frame of reference to do a complete turnaround in the early 1900^s, after the Art Nouveau movement? The bare aesthetics that had earlier been applied to unimportant warehouses became the standard for our homes and official buildings. Even though previously admired by both architects and users, traditional ornamentation and other artistic embellishment came to be considered kitschy and a sign of bad taste.

It is obvious that social factors had an impact on the breakthrough of Modernism. After World War I, people wanted to create a new, better world, and Modernism offered the right arguments irrespective of whether they were based on reality or not. We now know that Modernist apartments were no more functional or necessarily more affordable, but the clean, white surface, on a symbolic level, was successfully marketed as a sign of a better, modern society.

The architect Arata Isozaki describes Modernism as a clean surface onto which utopian ideas can be projected.

Utopia is literally a place of nowhere; however ideal, images and progressive movements can be projected on it. In order to induce utopia to ascend to the vacant position, Art, the erstwhile occupant, had to be removed: this marked the advent of the second crisis of architecture in the late nineteenth century (Isozaki 1995, xi).

Isozaki refers to the situation at the end of the 19th century, when art and ornamentation in buildings were considered part of the establishment and propaganda, which there was a reaction against.

To achieve the new aesthetic, it was important to create a convincing and straightforward process, one that would result in a clean – and better – surface.

Towards spirituality

As Modernism gathered strength in the early 20th century, visual arts, too, developed towards abstract expression. Most art historians consider the early 20th century pioneers of abstract art – Mondrian, Kandinsky, Kupka and Malevich – as representatives of this linear development, because they abandoned the figurative and narrative element in their art. To claim that their art is merely a development towards the abstract form is, however, an oversimplification. The truth is much more complex.

What is often forgotten is the fact that the above-mentioned pioneers' primary objective was not to play with colours and forms; instead, they wanted to "depict" spirituality, the fourth dimension or the geometry behind objects, each working within the context of theosophy. There is a deeper and, in a way, narrative meaning in their work, which is often ignored or considered uninteresting. Art historian Sixten Ringbom describes Kandinsky's fear of producing art that is abstract only in its form:

In his dread of the danger of ornament and "the dead semblance of stylized forms" he adopted occult claims that made non-representational painting not only an art movement but also an offshoot of mystical tradition (Ringbom 1986, 150).

Peter Cornell describes this connection in his book *Den hemliga källan*. He explains that the teaching at the Bauhaus, one of the intellectual fortresses of Modernism (until the school moved from Weimar to Dessau and Hannes Meyer became the director), was based on theosophical and medieval theories, a fact that is often ignored. According to Johannes Itten, one of the Bauhaus teachers with knowledge about esoteric theories, all lines and surface forms can be derived from one, two or three basic forms, with three worlds expressing themselves in these forms:

1. The solid, heavy material world in the square.
2. The spiritual sphere of sentiment and movement in the circle.
3. The intellectual world of logics, concentration, light and fire in the triangle.

For a spiritual person, these three symbols are not merely empty shapes but they symbolise God's great powers (Cornell 1981, 48).

Kandinsky's emotionally loaded view about depicting spiritual levels was contrasted by the more rational outlook of Mondrian and Theo van Doesburg. Harriett Watts defines the term "concrete art" coined by van Doesburg as "art conceived wholly in the mind without any formal information from nature or from the sentiments" (Watts 1986, 239).

With Plato's saying "God geometrises" as their starting point, they distanced themselves from nature, which was seen to be on a lower, chaotic level. An example of this is the absence of the colour green in Mondrian's abstract paintings.

My interpretation is that the interest in abstract forms that spread widely around the turn of the 20th century could not be based solely on the Machine Age and new technologies, but rather that the spiritual quest was equally important. Cornell also refers to Modernism in architecture without furthering the idea:

"I think that certain roots of functionalism and Le Corbusier could be found in this platonist soil" (Cornell 1981, 50).

We may ask whether the shift towards simplistic architecture would have been quite so smooth had architects not been supported by the leading contemporary visual artists.

Modernism's tendency to simplify this shift also resulted in a view that even layers that stretched far back in history were dated. Enthusiasm for the new produced some influential texts by such pioneers of Modernist architecture theory as Adolf Loos and Le Corbusier. They reject ornamentation in the form in which it had appeared in the history of architecture:

Tail pieces and garlands, exquisite ovals where triangular doves preen themselves or one another, boudoirs embellished with "poufs" in gold and black velvet, are now more than the intolerable witnesses to a dead spirit. These sanctuaries stifling with elegancies, or on the other hand with the follies of "Peasant art", are an offence (Le Corbusier 1986, 91).

Le Corbusier is also very clear about his opinion on the architectural process that leads to the abstract:

Civilizations advance. They pass through the age of the peasant, the soldier and the priest and attain what is rightly called culture. Culture is the flowering of the effort to select. Selection means rejection, pruning, cleansing; the clear and the naked emergence of the Essential (Ibid. 138).

Le Corbusier continues by claiming, like Adolf Loos, that ornamentation can only be found among simple races, and he describes cubes, spheres, cylinders and cones as essential building blocks in the creation of beauty in architecture. Genius is in the unique ability to achieve order and unity by measurement and to organise. For Le Corbusier, measurement is concrete, not the poetic measurement Heidegger talks about in his essay "...dichterisch wohnet der Mensch...". In his analysis of the text, Adam Sharr writes:

Heideggerian measuring involved listening. It could judge anything against anything. It might be done emotionally and instinctively, in a bodily and sensory way, or it could be more reflective and deliberate. The tools for measurement, in his scheme, were an individual's judgement, their imagination, their senses and emotions (Sharr 2007, 80).

It is interesting and somehow frightening to observe the polarity within Le Corbusier's psyche. In his wildest architectural plans, he wanted to demolish large parts of Paris' historic centre and replace them with 18 skyscrapers, a group of rectilinear buildings and enormous motorways (Jenger 1996, 49).

Even though these plans may be taken as provocation, it is not entirely certain that, given the chance, Le Corbusier would not have carried them out.

At the same time, his paintings done in private (he was a professionally trained painter and self-taught architect) moved from the strict constructivism apparent in his architecture towards a freer figurative idiom. We should, then, separate a built environment, which should be cold and mathematical, from art, which is limited by the frame of a painting or a sculpture and is more readily allowed to show emotion. Nature's chaos is seen to be alien to man's sophisticated spiritualism. A dualistic idea of man emerges.

The deeper one goes, the more complicated the issue becomes. Many later works by Le Corbusier have ornamental details and even pure decoration, manifesting a desire to combine the rational and poetic sides of his psyche. For instance, the housing development *Unité d'habitation* in Marseilles (1947–52), reminiscent of a sculpture installation, has large surfaces of ceramic tile ornaments. There are concrete imprints of the *Modulor* figure, based on Le Corbusier's "modulor" measurement unit, as decoration on the external walls. In fact, a number of Le Corbusier's famous buildings, the Ronchamp chapel in particular, have strong sculptural features, where rational straight lines give way to an organic idiom. In my opinion, Le Corbusier's desire to create a clean, faultless theoretical system is often in conflict with his practice: his sensitivity is clearly apparent in many of his buildings. Of course, this is partly due to Le Corbusier's evolution as an architect; he wrote his most significant texts decades before the above-mentioned buildings were constructed.

Many of the architects who were inspired by Le Corbusier's ideas forgot about his artistic side. This resulted in cold architecture, such as the Nokia office complex in Ruoholahti, Helsinki (2001), and most of the architectural designs produced in Finland over the past few decades.

In the *Life on a Leaf* project, I am working with architect Erkki Pitkäranta to restore the connection between artistic elements and building structure, as well as to gradually

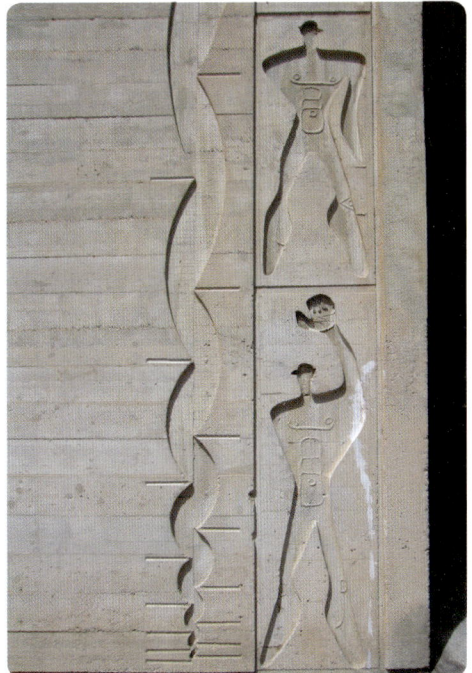

Le Corbusier: *Unité d'habitation*, Marseille (1947–52).

create a connection between man and nature through culture. First I need to clarify how I see the concept of art in relation to architecture.

What is architecture, what is art?

Immanuel Kant (1724–1804) discusses the concept of beauty in his book *Kritik der Urteilskraft* (1790). He divides beauty into two categories: "free beauties", which include, for example, flowers (so-called natural beauties), music that is not set to words and works of art. The other category is called "dependent beauties", which presuppose a concept. This has an effect on how the object is shaped, as well as how it is experienced. This category includes tattoos on people and all kinds of buildings, for example.

When we consider free beauty (and Kant specifically refers to the object's form as any adornment, such as colour, would be a distraction), even the judgment of beauty is pure:

> *There is presupposed no concept of any purpose, which the manifold of the given object is to serve, and which therefore is to be represented in it. By such a concept the freedom of the imagination which disports itself in the contemplation of the figure would only be limited (Kant 2000, 82).*

Kant does not include architecture in the category of free beauty, because when we look at a building, we always associate it with its function. According to Kant, ornamentation represents freer beauty than a building. "So also delineations à la grecque, foliage for borders or wall-papers, mean nothing in themselves; they represent nothing – no object under a definite concept – and are free beauties" (Ibid. 81).

For Kant, works of art and a building are separate elements, which can, however, interact to create an impressive building.

Like Kant, I think that artists and architects approach reality and their work from different angles. In the first place, or at least at a very early stage, an architect must consider the space plan, which must cover all functions required by the building. The architect also needs to be able to enlarge the scale and design repeatable modules so that a large space can be filled in an economically viable manner. Naturally, this also affects the architect's aesthetic taste.

An artist, on the other hand, is allowed to work with "the spatial designs of the psyche" and exact details. These may manifest themselves in abstract works of conceptual art or extremely small scale works that might nevertheless have a huge impact on the viewer. Many artists may find it difficult to increase up to the scale of a building's façade, for the very reason that the usual scale they are accustomed to is so different.

This, of course, does not prevent an architect from mastering even the tiniest details or an artist to handle the large scale. Michelangelo had no problems designing *Piazza del Campidoglio* in Rome. During the Art Nouveau period, architects were still taught drawing and ornamentation, and artists learnt their craft on a monumental scale as a great deal of their work consisted of decorating buildings. The Modernist view that each art form has its own unique essence and that each should seek its own perfection has brought about the situation we are in today, where both professions lead separate lives:

> *This process deprives architecture of all excess decoration and reduces it to a skeletal structure, stating above all else that architecture has nothing to do with art and should only be construction (Isozaki 1995, xi).*

This is the reason I would like to see whether integrating professional skills of an architect and an artist could result in new and surprising architectural outcomes. In order to be better able to examine this collaboration, I am taking the liberty of considering the artistic element separately from the architectural one.

Of course, there are many examples where these two categories overlap. A host of houses built in the 2000s that architectural theorist Charles Jencks calls "iconic buildings", for instance.

> *An iconic building, as we will see, has many and often divergent likenesses to the most bizarre and contradictory things. This is a reason they are often so powerful and amazing (as with Bilbao, above, "the building as a fish, mermaid, and artichoke") (Jencks 2005, 22).*

Jencks is referring here to the Guggenheim Museum in Bilbao by Frank Gehry, which is a typical example of an "iconic building". In Finland these are, often somewhat derogatorily, called "wow architecture".

I think these buildings are so sculptural in form that it could be said that the entire building is an ornamental detail, a jewel or sculpture. They could, thus, be regarded at least in part as "free beauties" as per Kant's categorisation. In other words, we can look at their sculptural form without thinking that they are buildings. For example, 30 St. Mary Axe in London (2000–2004), more commonly known as *The Gherkin* (and formerly known as the Swiss Re Building), designed by Norman Foster, may be seen as a sculpture from a distance. Other examples include the Kunsthaus Graz by Colin Fournier and Peter Cook (2001–2003) and most of Frank Gehry's buildings.

In my projects with Erkki Pitkäranta, I have tried to avoid the situation where an artistic element, such as a painting or a sculpture, is inserted into a

24H: *Accordion house*, Övre Gla, Sweden, 2003. Picture: Christian Richters.

Eugene Tsui: Tsui House, Matthews Street, Berkeley, 1995. Picture: Eugene Tsui.

Norman Foster: Swiss Re headquarters, 30 St. Mary Axe, London (2000–2004).

George Veronda: Main building and studio, 1979
Painting by Roger Brown.

completed building. If the artist and architect are already working together during the planning phase, the artistic element may be incorporated into the building's exterior form and the design of floors, walls, windows, décor and other details. This is how we approached our collaboration with the 20 artists who were invited to design artwork for the *Life on a Leaf* house.

The house and nature

Since I am interested in the various visual and symbolic ways that nature can relate to construction, I think I should explain how I understand the difference between living in a Modernist house and a house inspired by the Arts and Crafts movement.

When I visited Chicago in autumn 2004, I had a chance to spend a week at the home of the artist Roger Brown (1941–1997), to the east of Lake Michigan. The house, designed in 1979 by Brown's partner, the architect George Veronda, is a typical example of a Modernist house. And it is not too far from its inspiration: Mies van der Rohe's *Farnsworth House* (1946–51) is located in Plano, Illinois.

Immediately after that, I spent a month at Howard Shaw's house, designed in the spirit of Arts and Crafts, to the west of Lake Michigan, north of Chicago.

Arts and Crafts, which preceded Art Nouveau, emphasised the use of local materials, forms and traditions when producing contemporary architecture, art and handicrafts. The movement's most prominent artist was William Morris (1834–1896), who lifted textile arts to the status of a visual art form.

Veronda

Roger Brown (1941-97) was an inventive artist, whose ornamental, somewhat surrealist motifs may have made me expect a more imaginative house than the one George Veronda (1941–1984) had designed, but Veronda was Brown's partner, which obviously affected the choice of the architect. Besides, the white walls in the house act as a good background for Brown's paintings.

The house, or rather the complex with a main building, a guest house and a studio, lies on a beautiful site among green trees on the shores of Lake Michigan. The houses look like two boxes opposite each other. The short walls are completely made of glass so that one can see from one building into the other. The houses illustrate the Modernist way of thinking: all the rooms are on one level, which makes moving around easier. The windows are enormous, glass walls, really, so that one can observe the nature outside. The entire construction follows a strict plan, as do the planks of the ground-level bridge that connects the two houses. All the walls and ceilings have been painted white, and the interior walls form a backdrop for the collection of art and handicrafts.

After a week in the house, I was able to start making observations. The first concerns transparency. Modernists wanted to let as much light into houses as possible. This led to fitting in entire walls made of glass. There was even a group of architects in the early 20th century who called themselves the *Gläserne Kette* (*The Crystal Chain*), which included Hans Scharoun, Bruno Taut, Walter Gropius and Hermann Finsterlin. To them, glass had a strong symbolic significance: it represented the light, transparent and democratic society of the future (Kruft 1994, 373).

But the transparency of glass causes practical problems. The room I slept in has a glass wall that faces a bedroom in the other building, which has a similar

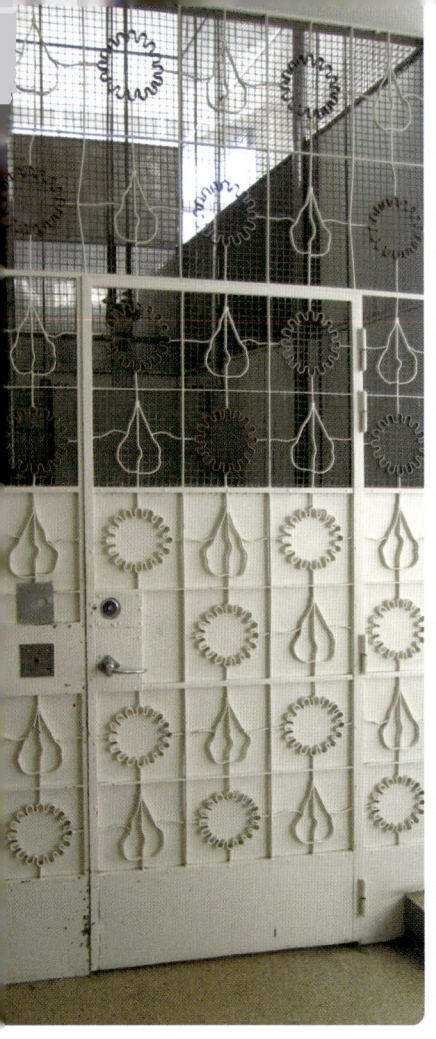

Ornamentation as a part of the structure. Lift at *Lastenlinna* Childrens' Hospital, Lastenlinnantie 2, Helsinki. Elsi Borg with Otto Flodin and Olavi Sorta, 1948.

Nature transforms into ornament. Louis Sullivan: Carson, Pirie, Scott and Company department store main entrance, Chicago, 1899.

Mickey Mouse transforms into ornament. The Disney Store, 717 North Michigan Avenue, Chicago. 1990s.

Casts of Catalonian bread used as ornament. Salvador Dalí museum, Figueres, 1974.

Ornamentation on the ceiling. Ödön Lechner and Gyula Pártos: The main entrance of the Museum for Applied Arts, Budapest, 1896.
The story as ornament. Johan Victor Strömberg: Kuopio market hall, 1902.
Ornament as a part of the structure. Door shelter photographed in Istanbul, 2008.

Burnham & Root: *The Rookery,* Chicago, 1888. Frank Lloyd Wright changed the lobby space in 1907. To create a space with more light he added light fixtures and surrounded the dark ornate cast iron columns with white marble with a golden pattern.

Nature itself as ornament. Wall planted by Gilles Clément and Patrick Blanc, Quai Branly Museum, Paris, 2006.

Nature-inspired ornament on the divideer between the inside space and nature outside. Marie Antoinette with architect Richard Mique: Pavilion in *Le Hameau*, Versailles, 1783.

Ludwig Mies van der Rohe: *Farnsworth House* (1946–51), Plano, Illinois. The curtains that partly cover the windows were installed, after a long quarrel, by the owner Edith Farnsworth against the wishes of Mies van der Rohe. The house was originally surrounded by untamed vegetation.

George Veronda: Main building and studio, 1979.

glass wall. This is well-suited to those with an exhibitionist streak, which may have been true of Brown and Veronda. But those concerned with maintaining their privacy must pull the roller blind down, thus blocking out all the light. A similar lack of privacy is also a feature in Mies van der Rohe's legendary *Farnsworth House*. Its first owner and commissioner Edith Farnsworth was constantly arguing with Mies van der Rohe because she did not want to live in a shop window. In an interview in House Beautiful in 1953, she said:

"Do I feel implacable calm?" she repeated. "The truth is that in this house with its four walls of glass I feel like sentinel on guard day and night. I can rarely strech out and relax...

...What else? I don't keep a garbage can under my sink. Do you know why? Because you can see the whole 'kitchen' from the road on the way in here and the can would spoil the appearance of the whole house. So I hide it in the closet farther down from the sink. Mies talks about 'free' space: but his space is very fixed. I can't even put a clothes hanger in my house without considering how it affects everything from the outside. Any arrangement of furniture becomes a major problem, because the house is transparent, like an X-ray." (Friedman 1996, 188).

Alice Friedman quotes this interview in the book Not at Home, which deals with how home life is suppressed in Modernist art and architecture. The quote may be a little exaggerated since Farnsworth lived in the house for twenty years, but it is an indication of how heated the argument was. Friedman also points to another, more female-oriented, view. Women have always reacted to the way men look at them and, unlike men, they have a greater need for private places out of the reach of men's stares. In his introduction to the book, Christopher Reed claims that Modernist architecture was hostile to the traditional understanding of home. According to him, it was a design for the "modern" successful man, who in the early 20th century was still locked in the "old" bourgeois architecture despite the fact that the society required something else (Reed 1996, 9).

I can almost hear Le Corbusier shouting: "We claim, in the name of the steamship, of the airplane and of the motorcar, the right to health, logic, daring, harmony, perfection" (Le Corbusier 1986, 19).

The other observation concerns the house's relationship with the surrounding nature. Because of the enormous glass walls, nature is not merely an amazing spectacle but also an intruder in Brown's main building. Nature is present all the time in a way I find a little annoying. Yet the building's geometric box-like form is as far removed from nature's organic forms as possible. This creates a conflict: the architectural idiom refers to rational technology and nature's organic forms are pushed aside, but at the same time nature is, visually, allowed indoors, making it hard to keep away. This impression is strengthened by the fact that the surrounding area is left in a completely or almost completely natural state. There is no garden-like area between the house and wild vegetation. This appears to be a conscious feature among Modernists. It applies to *Farnsworth House* too, which was originally surrounded by high vegetation, and the house that is possibly the most famous of Le Corbusier's designs, *Villa Savoye*, in Poissy (1929–31), which is situated right in the midst of nature. "The view is very beautiful, the grass is a beautiful thing, the forest as well: one must touch them as little as possible" (Menin 2003, 125).

Even if the experience of nature is overwhelming, the view from out the windows feels like standing behind a camera or looking at a screen. Beatriz Colomina describes Le Corbusier's houses as

... a device to see the world, a mechanism for viewing. Shelter, separation from the outside, is provided by the window's ability to turn the threatening world outside the house into a reassuring picture. The inhabitant is enveloped, wrapped, protected by the pictures (Colomina 1994, 7).

My third observation is about the exterior walls. Modernist houses that have been painted white soon start to look badly weathered if they are not maintained. This is even more apparent in South America, for example in São Paulo, Brazil, where the white walls of many gigantic building projects have cracked and filled with wild plants. The house designed by Veronda is not constructed particularly well, which makes it even more important that its small details should be carefully maintained to make them work aesthetically.

The white walls of Veronda's house distance themselves from ornamentation (ignoring the replaceable works of art that hang on the walls as ornaments), although the network of iron girders on the ceiling has the same effect as ornamentation, making the building more mentally accessible.

Despite being a "functional" building, it has details that make living in it less comfortable. For example, the porch roof is a design made of wooden laths that follows the rhythm of the building. However, the porch is not covered, which means that when it rains, one gets wet.

One of the original Modernist ideas was to integrate works of art into buildings; not into structures themselves, but as replaceable elements on interior walls. The point was to provide artworks a virgin white background surface where they would stand out. Today's Modernism no longer manages to achieve this; it actually seems to encourage keeping art away, embellishing clean wall surfaces with abstract architectural details.

George Veronda: Main building and studio, 1979. Roger Brown's art collection.

In this sense, Veronda's house follows the original Modernist principle. Its walls are a stage for Roger Brown's collection of outsider and folk art that makes the house bloom. A fine collection of Brown's own work is also displayed in the house. We can see the blackened Puerto Rican face of the palm tree sculpture, switch on a night lamp with a stem carved like a shark's head or study Brown's family tree installation that proves he is related to Elvis.

The works of art are exhibited as if in a museum of modern art, with the underlying idea that they are as separate from their surroundings as possible, yet in communication with nature through the big windows.

Shaw

The great emphasis on art is a connecting feature between Veronda's house and Howard Shaw's (1869–1926) house in Ragdale. Shaw's house is also filled with works and objects of art both inside and outside. Shaw collected some of these works on his travels, while others were made by members of his family, some of whom were artists, sculptors or poets. The ambience created by the pieces is as wild as that from Brown's collection, but Shaw's art and objects belong to the building. All the details work together to create a total work of art that follows the principles of the Arts and Crafts movement.

Shaw was an architect who had a fantastic ability to mix Greek pillars with the cottage style. Arts and Crafts, like Art Nouveau afterwards, took the indoors as its starting point in building. So if Shaw needed yet another veranda on the roof, he built it without worrying too much about the proportions. The outcome was a house that many architects criticise and do not consider to be architecture at all.

Staying at Shaw's house was like being on an expedition. Every day I was able to find new details, new viewpoints, new wallpaper patterns or poems incised into a stone in the garden. The house is a great adventure

Howard Shaw's house. Ragdale, 1898.

and really succeeded in stirring my imagination and creative energy. The windows are small and provide the required privacy, but there are also huge conservatories filled with flowers, where you can read in a peaceful, lush environment.

Where Roger Brown's house is surrounded by untamed nature, Shaw's house has a landscaped park, which continues far into the prairie. Shaw was very particular about the views from the house, and each branch to be cut had to be discussed with the house's inhabitants. He acquired a long plot of the prairie in order to have a view over the wilderness. The site remains a natural park, ringed by wide motorways that are invisible, although not silent.

I can draw the following conclusions: the big difference between Veronda's house and Shaw's is their attitude towards nature. The Arts and Crafts style, with its numerous architectural surprises, details and hiding places, resembles nature's way of organising without any strict geometry.

Another element that distinguishes Shaw's house from Veronda's is ornamentation. Various wallpaper surfaces with organic motifs refer to the surrounding environment and gently make us aware of it. There, we are not standing behind huge Modernist camera windows looking at nature; instead, we are connected to it through gradual changes from relatively untouched nature to a park-like site, to the interior ornamentation based on natural forms and finally to our own bodies. The building symbolises a wish to be part of nature's cycle as opposed to an interruption to it, and it can be seen as a tangible expression of this wish. The Arts and Crafts movement held local elements in very high esteem. Alice Hayes and Susan Moon (1990) describe life in Shaw's house and show how local elements were important both in the choice of materials for the house, as well as in the theatre built in the surrounding park where local amateur actors performed.

Howard Shaw's house. Ragdale, 1898.

Aalto and Le Corbusier

In contrast to my opinion that Modernism, on the symbolic level, represents an anti-nature viewpoint, many leading practitioners of Modernism emphasise their strong personal relationship with nature and their intention to bring nature into Modernist architectural spaces.

Many buildings designed by Alvar Aalto, for example, show his strong desire to incorporate organic elements into them. In an interview from 1968, Aalto said that he was more interested in Art Nouveau than in Bauhaus (Menin & Samuel 2003, 61), although he progressed towards a kind of Modernist architecture that prefers strict geometry and distances itself from organic forms. Among Aalto's work, the Enzo Gutzeit headquarters in Helsinki (1962) is an example of this development.

In their study of Aalto's and Le Corbusier's relationship with nature, *Nature and Space: Aalto and Le Corbusier*, Sarah Menin and Flora Samuel show how Le Corbusier referred to nature and its structures, e.g. the heart and the leaf, in order to create "radiant" architecture with harmonic geometry as its starting point. According to Le Corbusier, images of the numerical world were projected onto the spatial world: first by nature itself, then by men and above all by artists. By creating modular systems based on harmonic measurements of human body, it was possible to create architecture that would bring happiness to an age of confusion (ibid., 64–69).

Aalto was more critical of the search for the perfect module. In a speech made in 1957, Aalto said that the search for a module represents the slavery of human beings to technical futilities that in themselves do not contain one iota of real humanity. When he was asked what his studio's module was, he replied, "One millimetre or less." Aalto was truly interested in using nature as a point of reference, not in copying it or representing it (ibid., 69).

Both Aalto and Le Corbusier wanted to blur the line between nature and a building's interior, but in different ways and with different results. Aalto wanted the outside to inhabit the interior of buildings, as demonstrated in his use of internal piazzas, for example. Le Corbusier, on the other hand, built towards the exterior: porches, roof garden rooms and other spaces for nature to settle in. His view resulted in more sterile interiors than those of Aalto's (ibid., 72).

Aalto thought that man was above nature and that man's intervention with nature need not be harmful – quite the opposite. He said that although not an inch of ground remained intact in Italy, there was no lack of scenic beauty. The problem was not a matter of "conserving nature" or a return to wilderness, but rather a matter of culture and taste as well as understanding man's relationship with nature (ibid., 76).

I think that Le Corbusier presumed that "sacred geometry" was the basis of all art and architecture. For him, the way to happiness was to distil out this geometry. Many architects still agree with this view. For a building's design to be architecture, it must be founded on geometric harmony. Based on this view, anything that disturbs the abstract geometry, such as traditional ornaments, is peeled off. It also says that the essence of architecture is abstract and a building should not refer to an object such as a hat or a leaf, or even represent it. But as I discussed earlier, Le Corbusier, contrary to his earlier texts, used a great deal of ornamentation in his post-war designs.

Aalto's view of nature's role in architecture could be summarised thus:

1. To lend forms to architecture.
2. To illustrate materials and examples of cell division.
3. To maintain and enrich life in the psychological realm.

Aalto did not often construct buildings from wood, but instead used it in interiors to give buildings a unique character. He emphasised wood's importance to mental health. Furthermore, Aalto was reluctant to use steel and concrete in interior design since these materials were not satisfactory from a human point of view (ibid., 78–79).

Minimalism and nature

There are architects who base their work on Modernist tradition that highlights the positive relationship between architecture and nature.

Japanese architect Tadao Ando (born in 1941) believes in minimalist form as a source of tension and a spiritual threshold between man and nature. Japanese tradition seeks to find a union between man and nature; human life should not oppose nature, but draw it into an intimate association. A geometric form in itself is lifeless, but comes alive when human life and nature come together within it. Water, wind, light and sky bring architecture that is based on transparent logic onto the ground level of reality and awaken the manmade life within it.

Ando thinks that a simple geometric form creates tension through which nature can be experienced. Architecture transforms nature, changes its meaning, through abstraction (Ando 1996, 460).

Ando agrees with Le Corbusier in his view that nature is more prominent when seen from a geometrically clean space. Veronda's architecture in Roger Brown's house relies on this, as do numerous art museums, e.g. the Louisiana Museum of Modern Art in Humlebæk, Denmark, and the Sara Hildén Art Museum in Tampere, Finland. Visitors can look at the aestheticised – or spiritualised, as many call it – nature through floor to ceiling windows that punctuate the world of artworks.

Alvar Aalto: Paimio sanatorium, 1929–33.

Alvar Aalto: Worker's association building, Jyväskylä, 1925.

Tadao Ando: *Honpuku Temple* (water temple), 1991. Photo: Wikimedia Commons.

The Life on a Leaf house's connection to nature

I would say that the ability of Shaw's Arts and Crafts house and many Art Nouveau houses to gradually bring nature indoors is a feature of different quality. There is none of the aesthetising tension Ando mentions in these houses, but instead continuous contact through an axis: the surrounding, "wild" nature is linked to a park-like, well-tended area, which is linked to small window squares and curtains with flower patterns, and finally through the flowers on the wallpaper through to the human consciousness. The connection is made smoothly rather than through a stark contrast. I think that this allows us to be ONE with nature, and here cultural elements are extremely important means of communication.

In the *Life on a Leaf* project, Erkki Pitkäranta and I will take a step towards creating a more complex and continuous aesthetic transformation from nature to indoors. Instead of using just a geometric form in the house, we will mix geometry with one natural form – a leaf – and use this as the basis for the ground plan, and instead of installing rectangular windows, we will use organic forms such as the leaf or a drop of water.

We will not stop there, though. We want the house to convey the experience of walking along a forest path. Walking along the curved walls on the ground floor is a completely different experience from doing the same within a rectangular room. The load-bearing pillars and the chimney flue look like abstract tree trunks, with the narrow vertical windows on the first floor, letting light shine in like between real trees in a forest. Each of the three storeys has their own unique ambience. It could be described as climbing from the bottom of a valley up onto a mountain.

Our aim is also to introduce nature into the interior through the use of ornamentation and works of art. The motifs for the dandelion ornaments on the concrete walls and the floor pattern on the first floor, for example, were found in the apple orchard outside the house.

The sound installation by Shawn Decker that is integrated into the ornamental railing on the concrete bridge also brings nature indoors and creates virtual nature in the house. There are about thirty small speakers that are part of the railing's ornamental surface, and they each have their own computer generated crunching sound, which is based on rhythms in nature. The sensors on the exterior walls register the wind speed and slight changes in light and send signals to the computer that controls the sound installation. This ensures that the soundscape in the heart of the house changes with nature, much in the same way as changes in weather make old houses creak.

Although the *Life on a Leaf* project has been inspired by the Art Nouveau movement, our intention is not to imitate its style, but to further develop its principles.

As far as I am aware, Art Nouveau architects did not use natural forms as the basis of spatial design, but instead integrated forms from nature into the traditional spatial model, i.e. the cube. This is the reason I think it is important to examine how the starting point for the *Life on a Leaf* house, the leaf form, works as a living environment. I want to see if organic forms are functional in a home as well. I will also make a subjective study of how the inhabitants' mental health is influenced by the more direct visual and emotional connection to nature, which was man's original habitat, since our genetic makeup has not changed radically since the Stone Age.

On a superficial level, Art Nouveau may be seen as a rather conservative movement with emphasis on the past, one that claims that the home

Ornament as sound, as a railing, on the floor and as a fabric pattern. Rosegarden Art & Architecture (Jan-Erik Andersson and Erkki Pitkäranta): *Life on a Leaf House*, Turku (2006–09).

should be an oasis of peace and beauty. Stephen Escritt, however, writes in *Art Nouveau*:

> …*public vigour and private peace were not seen as mutually exclusive, quite the opposite: contemporary theories on the role of the home in the modern world suggested that an active public life needed to be sustained by an aesthetically pleasing, comfortable domestic environment (Escritt 2000, 83–84).*

In my opinion, Art Nouveau's idea of the home as not only a shelter for the inhabitant's inner thoughts, but also as a source of inspiration, encompasses the aim of reaching one's mental space. The décor should not be a reminder of the concrete external reality, but should encourage subjective escape.

This leads one to think the feminine shelter of the womb, and the concept of femininity is, indeed, often attributed to Art Nouveau. From this, it is easy to draw the conclusion that Modernism was a masculine and rational reaction to Art Nouveau.

Now, a hundred years after Art Nouveau's heyday, nature has reacted and informed us that we are causing enormous changes in ecosystems. We have been forced to re-evaluate the Modernist linear developmental optimism, and this should also be evident in architecture. In the wake of the Modernist view of architecture, there are demands for more minimalist architecture as all "unnecessary ornamentation" is expensive, and from an ecological perspective as well. The architect Jukka Paaso argues against the *Life on a Leaf* house in his polemic:

> *In my opinion, Andersson's house does not meet all social, ethical and ecological requirements of architecture […] I find it sad that in these dramatic times of climate change someone in Turku starts launching unsustainable image fantasies (Paaso 2008, 15).*

I, for one, believe that we can learn a lot from the opposing view: a playful and enjoyable cityscape with plenty of ornaments and organic forms makes life more relaxed and reduces energy consumption as there is less need to travel to tourist resorts by plane or to summer cottages by car. Ornamentation is also about caring, looking, wondering and slowing down: it is about energies that should be rediscovered.

Ornament on the border between heaven and earth. Rosegarden Art & Architecture (Jan-Erik Andersson and Erkki Pitkäranta): *Life on a Leaf* -House, Turku (2006–09).

Ornament on the border between heaven and earth. Photo taken in York, 2011.

> "Although ornament is most properly only an accessory to architecture, and should never be allowed to usurp the place of structural features, or to overload or to disguise them, it is in all cases the very soul of an architectural monument."
>
> Owen Jones,
> *The Grammar of Ornament*, 1856

Zincirlikuyu cemetery, Levent, Istanbul, photographed in 2008.

Ornament as a building's soul

In the 20th and 21st centuries, the debate about architecture mainly dealt – and continues to deal – with ornamentation's role in a building. Should it be removed altogether or turned into some technical elements, or do we want to see buildings that are huge sculptures, which some people would be happy to call ornaments?

To provide some background for these standpoints, we should discuss the terms ornament and decoration.

Adolf Loos

Modernism, the style that dominated the 20th century architecture, questioned the connection between decorative elements and everyday objects, including buildings. One of the most prominent representatives of Modernism, the Austrian architect and theorist Adolf Loos (1870-1933) went so far as to liken ornamentation to a crime in his influential essay *Ornament und Verbrechen* (1908). To decorate and to create ornaments was typical of lower races. They were a primitive means of expression that should be abandoned on the way to a better future for humankind. Loos describes how the walls of our houses will glow white like in Zion, the capital of heaven. Loos comforts those who were worried about the age of machines only producing insensitive ornamentation by praising his own industrialised century for being *incapable* of producing ornamentation. (Loos 1908, 288–289).

Loos' text is highly polemical and contains arguments that are hard to take seriously, such as the claim that if a modern person has a tattoo, he or she is either a criminal or a degenerate. He continues by saying that if a tattooed person dies at liberty, it means that he only died a few years before he could commit a murder! (ibid., 288).

There are, however, some relevant arguments in the text that I must comment on if I want to defend ornamentation. The most serious of these states that ornamentation is a waste of material, time and money. Instead of spending resources on producing ornamentation, we should spend the time we have saved on cultural pursuits (ibid., 290). Loos feels sorry for his cobbler, who cannot go listen to Beethoven because he has to sit at home and decorate shoes for very little money (ibid., 294).

Now, a hundred years later, I think that Modernism has been very successful in its mission to educate people to appreciate clean and ornament-free surfaces. "Scandinavian Coolness" is a good example in the field of design. The early 21st century has, however, witnessed a new interest in ornamentation, particularly among young interior designers.

This renewed interest is partly due to the fact that people want to have a cosy nest, where they can escape the world's problems, much in the way Art Nouveau was a reaction to industrialism. Another reason is that it is now possible to both design and produce ornaments using computer applications, which keeps the prices down.

On my travels to Istanbul, I have experienced the beauty and the mastery of detail and surface that is visible in the ornamentation on mosques. This is why I find it very hard to agree with Loos, who thought that ornamentation was barbaric. We could also approach the issue from the opposing side: the 14th century Islamic philosopher and historian Ibn Khaldun saw the degree of "refinement" (by which he probably meant complexity) in a work of craft as relating to the degree of civilization in a given society (Blair & Bloom 2004, 125).

Many of Loos' arguments have also been proven wrong. It is often as expensive, if not more expensive, to construct a minimalist building by hiding all necessary details (such as ventilation ducts and outlet pipes) under a clean, ornament-free surface. "In fact less was more work," says architect and theorist Robert Venturi (Venturi & al. 1977, 114).

One famous example is the white Italian marble cladding on Alvar Aalto's Finlandia Hall in Helsinki (1967–71), which had to be replaced recently as it is not suitable for the Finnish climate. As a matter of fact, it will need to be replaced again in a few years' time. Had it been made of Finnish granite instead, it would have been considerably cheaper and more durable.

Loos also ignored the fact that artisans may be happy to spend a few extra hours working to create an interesting surface. It may be a more difficult and arduous task, but finishing it can be very satisfying indeed.

Definition of ornament/decoration

In *The Nature of Ornament*, Kent Bloomer tries to identify the origin of ornament. According to Bloomer, the word *ornament* is derived from the Latin word *ornamentum*, rooted in *ornare*. This could be translated to mean "to confer grace upon some ceremonial object". The term ornament also has its origins within the Greek term *Kosmos*, which meant something like "universe", "order" and "ornament". For the ancient Greeks, *Kosmos* was the opposite of *Chaos*, and Eros was a prerequisite for creating *Kosmos* from Chaos. Bloomer says that "ornament" can thus be said to be a force that transforms conflicting wordly elements (Bloomer 2000, 15–17).

Bloomer continues examining the term *Kosmos* and finds a graceful connection to femininity: The Greek word kosmeo means "to arrange" and "to adorn". A woman *kosmése* (adorns) herself in order to make her *Kosmos* visible. Cities adorn themselves as well. An ornamented temple is one that is prepared to honour the god. (ibid., 17–18).

In the 20th century the terms *ornament* and *decoration* became separate. Ornament was understood to be linked with architecture, provide support for it, and thus somehow be acceptable. Decoration was simply a negative feature, a ruffle on the surface with no connection to the structure.

Bloomer's reasoning perhaps has traces of this spirit. He considers ornament as an art form and distinguishes it from decorative and other forms of art. Bloomer recognises certain attributes in ornament (ibid., 9–10). I summarise this as follows:

1. It is driven by lines rather than mass, space, texture, colour, materiality or portraiture, though all these properties contribute to its visibility.
2. Ornament's organisation is rhythmic. Geometry and proportion are subordinate elements.
3. At the same time, the statics of geometry and proportion are critical to the syntax between ornament and the object/building it embellishes.
4. If we think of ornament as a figuration that is dependent on multiple criteria, then one of these criteria must be the utilitarian form of its objects.
5. However, ornament also represents things and actions that do not originate in utility. Its meanings, therefore, are essentially combinational, and its figures tend to become metamorphoses (plants are merged with animals, etc).
6. The vitality, playfulness and fantasticality of ornament exist in the liminal or transitional space of its object (such as curtains that represent the transition between the walls and the surrounding landscape; my comment).

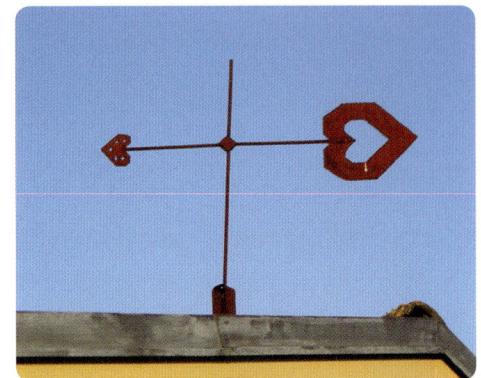

Ornament on the border between heaven and earth. Photographed in Laukaa, 2004.

Mechanical structure as ornament. The openings expand or contract depending on the strength of the sunlight. Jean Nouvel: Institute du Monde Arabe, Paris, 1987.

Ornament as a structural element. The roof of the *Church on Spilled Blood*, St Petersburg, 1883-1907.

Colour as ornament. Facade on apartment building in Sopot, 2010.

Ornate column. The Metropole Hotel, King Street, Leeds, 1800s.

Ornate column. The Disney Store, 717 North Michigan Avenue, Chicago, 1990s.

Bloomer wants to create a syntax for ornament and to give it status as one of the languages of humankind.

Brent C. Brolin states in his book *Architectural Ornament, Banishment & Return* that the difference between ornament and decoration is artificial, and he uses the terms interchangeably. He defines ornamentation by two characteristics that most people can agree on (Brolin 2000, 183–190), which I summarise as follows:

1. Ornament/decoration is something that is intentional and that embellishes as well. Thus a statue in a museum is not necessarily an ornament, but if it is placed on a building's façade, it "ornaments" it.
2. Ornament/decoration imposes some kind of visual order on the thing it embellishes.

To say that a certain kind of decoration would be better suited to the structure of a building is hindsight wisdom. An ornament that somehow seems to highlight the structure of a building is coincidental. It just fitted the Modernist movement view that ornament was an organic part of the building, whereas decoration had no relationship to it. Thus ornament must be taken seriously. Both are, in fact, equally nonessential from the structural point of view. It is the eye of the beholder, not an ideological opinion, that decides whether an ornament is beautiful or not. (The most orthodox choices made by Modernists were based on the new idea of beauty, new style, and had nothing to do with superior functionality or higher moral).

Ernst Gombrich turned to prehistoric man in his search for the roots of ornament. In his book *The Sense of Order*, he writes that the process of decoration is preceded by collecting the material, which is then arranged into shapes, and the arrangement must be fixed to some kind of support or base. After this, we can call it decoration. A decorated or painted human body is certainly one of the earliest examples (Gombrich 1979, 65).

Gombrich also writes about a hierarchical arrangement that presupposes two distinct steps: framing and filling. The first delimits the field and the other organises the resultant space. If there is a grid and the squares are filled with drawn or painted design, these together constitute the ornament (ibid., 75).

Fully aware that there are different opinions about the definitions of ornament and decoration, as well as about the question of whether they are interchangeable, I will be using the term ornamentation from now on, as it has a more favourable connotation than decoration.

Ornaments of Modernism

Even though Adolf Loos wrote essays to criticise ornamentation and distanced himself from the abundance of ornamentation that was common in the 19th century, he cannot be said to have left his buildings completely without ornaments. Quite the opposite: there are numerous carefully worked details and surfaces created from various types of marble.

In his book *Ornament. A Modern Perspective*, James Trilling comments on Loos' Goldman & Salatsch building in Vienna, also known as *Looshaus*. He sees the marble elements on the building's exterior walls as abstract ornaments placed at street level. To ensure that these ornaments made a proper impact, Loos left the upper storeys even simpler (Trilling 2003, 218).

> Loos did not always practice what he preached. The four columns of the Looshaus facade are non-functional – they carry no weight – yet they are made of solid marble. This is hardly a model of economy, but Loos was being

Ornament on the border between heaven and earth. Bowls for serving food to the gods:

Unter Den Linden, Berlin. Photographed in 2002.
Viiskulma, Helsinki. Photographed in 2002.
Ruissalo folk park. Photographed in 2002.
Versailles. Photographed in 2006.

capricious. He needed uninterrupted surface effects. Flat surfaces could be clad in a thin layer of marble, but a round column could not. For the ornament to be continuous, the column had to be cut from a single piece of stone (ibid.).

Trilling also states that when the human touch is removed from architecture, it is nature that provides Loos' architecture with an enlivening and spontaneous element, i.e. the patterns on the marble cladding and columns (ibid).

According to Brolin, Modernists did not actually abandon ornament, but channelled it into non-traditional media (Brolin 2000, 202). He mentions as an example Mies van der Rohe's Barcelona Pavilion (1928–9), which is considered as one the pioneering works of Modernist architecture. Mies van der Rohe removed all traditional ornaments from the surface, but the marble cladding he used has strong ornamental patterns.

I'd like to add here that the marble slabs are arranged side by side so that the patterns form mirror images, thus creating a kind of Rorschach inkblot image. I have seen similarly executed wall surfaces in the Hagia Sofia and the Chora Church in Istanbul.

To Brolin, it does not make much difference whether Mies van der Rohe chooses a particular piece of marble with beautiful colours and veins, cuts it into geometric forms and polishes them to silken finish or if a skilled artisan produces a brilliant imitation marble wall in a church in Bavaria.

If we can filter out the impact of decades of ornament phobia and look at these two buildings [Barcelona Pavilion and Bavarian church] with an unprejudiced eye, we can see that their architects took much the same kind of pleasure in embellishment. The difference is one of degree, not kind (ibid., 199).

In general, Modernists were – and are – very careful when choosing their materials. The choice is seldom based on function, but rather taste and preference. Modernist architecture is, in other words, a style among a number of styles. When an architect chooses it as his or her means of expression, it is a choice of style. "Designers claiming to search for a style of our time really mean 'a style I like'. It is another weapon to use against those whose vision of our times differs from that of the designer" (ibid., 237).

"New" materials do not demand new (Modernist) forms. Steel and concrete adapted themselves to decorative Art Deco architecture in the early 20th century, while Brolin also reminds us that the Romans invented concrete over 2,000 years ago (ibid., 181).

Gombrich also shows that this is not a new issue. He used Goethe's poem *Herrmann und Dorothea* (1797) as a funny example. In his poem, Goethe comments on the middle class's "sophisticated" taste after the French Revolution. The apothecary mourns his decorated garden pavilion and finally says he now wants something "tasteful". Everything has to be painted white, simple and smooth, with no carving or gilding. Imported wood, the most expensive kind, is fashionable now.

With this reference to the expensive imported wood used for these "simple" panellings, Goethe surely and subtly points to the sociological qualifications of the new purism. The lack of decoration and ornamentation must be compensated for by noble materials and exquisite craftmanship which proclaims at once that discriminating simplicity is a matter of choice and has nothing to do with lack of means. One might almost say that the more simple the shape the more careful must be the handling of the surfaces and the more choice the material (Gombrich 1979, 30–31).

Ornamentation with marble patterns. Photographed in Chora (Kariye Camii), a medieval church, Istanbul, 2008.

Ornamentation with marble patterns. Photographed in the Byzantine Church of Hagia Sofia, Istanbul, 2006.

Ornamentation with marble patterns. Photographed in Ludwig Mies van der Rohe's *Barcelona Pavilion* (1928–29). Destroyed in 1930, rebuilt in 1986.

Adolf Loos: Goldman & Salatsch building (*Looshaus*), Michaelerplatz, Vienna, 1910. Photo: Wikimedia Commons, Alexander Mayrhofer.

These examples prove that the transition from Art Nouveau to Modernism was really a transition from one style to another. The lack of traditional ornamentation had to be compensated by the use of luxurious materials. The finish of a surface and the choice of material are qualities that vulgarity and undefinability cannot reach; thus they become the signs of "true sophistication".

Referring to the famous 19th century theorist John Ruskin, Brolin says that a large number of works of art are produced to fit a particular place and can thus be considered decorative, for example Michelangelo's paintings on the Sistine Chapel ceiling (Brolin 2000, 190–191).

We need to be prepared to extend the concept of ornament into the other direction too, so that it also covers the architectural details that are popular among Modernists. Over the past ten years, a number of large horizontal grill structures, made of timber or aluminium, have been attached to the façades of building in Finland. A typical example of a 2000s building is the *Sanoma House* in the Helsinki city centre, which has a large, deep extra front that looks very technical and "functional". Architect Antti-Matti Siikala said that the grid is there to provide shelter from the sun (Siikala at my seminar, Galleria Sculptor, May 2003). Despite his explanation, I still think that its primary function is ornamental; a functional sun shade would not require this kind of scale.

According to Brolin, Modernist theories that architecture free from decoration is better suited to modern man's requirements of having a healthier and more functional environment – giving it the moral upper hand compared to other styles – have no basis in reality. Modernist arguments were identical to those presented by Augustus Pugin as early as the 19th century, and emphasise four principles (Brolin 2000, 94), which I summarise as follows:

1. The honest expression of structure. The structure of a building or an object should be emphasized, not disguised.
2. The honest expression of function. The purpose of the building or object should be apparent from looking at it.
3. The honest expression of materials. One material should not pretend to be another. The physical characteristics of a material should determine the techniques used to work it and the appearance of the final product.
4. The honest expression of the spirit of the times. The character of one's time can be captured in the design of an object or a building, and the designer has an intuitive understanding of what this character is.

What is remarkable is the fact that even if their theoretical framework was the same, Modernists ended up producing architecture that was as minimalist as possible, whereas Pugin's style was Neo-Gothic!

Brolin says that Modernists wanted to create a new style that would be distinguished from "bad taste", which some had tried to "cure" in various ways, including by means of art education, as early as the 19th century, but to no avail. The use of moral arguments was supposed to make the Modernist style indisputable.

Thus Modernism barricaded itself behind the four arguments mentioned above, which were based on something other than taste. There may be dispute when it comes to tastes, but we have no means to judge whose taste is better. Although we could tell "whether an object honestly reveals its function".

Even though Modernist details and material choices could be called ornaments – at least if we define ornament more broadly – there are major differences between these and traditional ornaments. Brolin says that the essence and the power of the traditional ornament lay in its variety of scale, ranging

Ornamentation with constructional elements. Ian Simpson Architects. Urbis: The Museum of the Modern City, Manchester, 2002.

from small rosettes to monumental frescos that offer something to excite the eye close up as well as from far away (ibid., 205).

I would like to add that ornament's symbolic content is different. Modernist ornaments symbolise technology and keep their distance from representational elements connected to the world of imagination and fairy tales.

An artist as a genius

Brolin points out that it was Kant's ideas of an artist as a genius, presented in the book *Critique of Judgment*, (*Kritik der Urteilskraft*, published in 1790), that institutionalised the separation of "fine arts" and craft (ibid., 19).

Before this, an artist and an artisan had shared a similar social status. Patrons and artists/artisans had had quite similar tastes until the 18th century. It was only during the period of industrialisation in the 19th century, when a wider arts market developed, that it could be said that artists' taste began to become distinct to that of the buyers'. This culminated in the idea of an artist as an original genius. It was questioned whether an artist could be a true artist if the general public liked his or her work (Brolin 2000, 68).

Brolin writes that this view resulted in a situation where those artists, artisans and architects who borrowed from previous styles were accused of lacking in originality – one was only a true artist if capable of creating something that was radically unconventional. The argument that an artist represented morally superior "good taste", as opposed to the public's "bad taste", justified the genius status of the artist and later, in the 20th century, it justified the entire art world! This can be used to justify Modernism distancing itself from "past styles" so that something "new" could be found.

While artists were beginning to be considered geniuses, decorative crafts were also starting to gain a better status in the late 19th century. Because of this, people started talking about good design and bad design, the latter of which was usually represented by popular taste. This process reached its climax in the new art theory launched by the leader of the Arts and Crafts movement, William Morris (1834–96), who thought that nothing could be a work of art that was not useful! He thus equated decorative and fine art (ibid., 105).

This led to a growing interest in the abstract and an undervaluation of representative elements in painting and ornamentation. The essence of a representative image was searched more thoroughly – "behind" the picture – to find a deeper meaning or sensation.

The concept of art was also redefined at the same time: the definitions of beauty and ugliness were simply swapped. Beauty had been connected to forms derived from nature and history; now these concepts became synonymous with ugliness and aesthetic degeneracy. Industrial and technological forms, which had earlier been considered epitomes of ugliness, became the measure of beauty in the new era (Brolin 2000, 153).

Robert Venturi et al. agree: "Modern architects began to make the back the front, symbolizing the configuration of the shed to create a vocabulary for their architecture" (Venturi & al. 1977, 114).

Ornamentation in the Modernist spirit:

Peter Bieber, Arvi Ilonen, Sulo Savolainen and Unto Toikkanen: Merihaka, Helsinki (1973–1975).

Paatero & Paatero: Turku University Hospital, 2012.

Postmodern ornament

In 1970s and 1980s, Postmodernist architecture tried to reintroduce elements dismissed by Modernism, although since then architecture has generally returned to Modernism's principles.

Ornamentation on the facade of an apartment building in Istanbul, 2008.

Ornament as an illusion. The lighter parts of the facade of the apartment building are painted to look that they are protruding from the facade. Photo taken in Chicago in 2005.

Ornamentation as a part of the structure.

Burglary shelter. Vieques, Puerto Rico. Photo taken in 2002.

There are many buildings with roof windows that look like eyes in Sibiu, Romania. Photo taken in 2007.

Rennie Mackintosh: Facade of Queen's Cross Church, Glasgow, 1899.

Ornament as an artwork. The artwork as an ornament. The door of artist Kosti Ahonen's house in Lahti, photographed in 2006.

Ornament as information. The facade of a poultry farm. Photographed along a country road in Southern Finland, 2006.

Ornament for a specific place. Building by the shore of Cony Island, New York. Photographed in 2007.

Lars Sonck: Hällberg summer cottage, 1897. Transferred and now used as the ÅSS Pavilion in Mariehamn, Åland.

Postmodernism did, however, leave a legacy of interest in ornamentation and alternative methods of construction. In his books *Complexity and Contradiction in Architecture* and *Learning from Las Vegas* (co-written by Denise Scott Brown and David Izenour), the architect and theorist Robert Venturi armed Modernism's opponents with intellectual artillery for presenting different ways of thinking. To put it simply, we could say that Venturi sought inspiration in "popular" architecture, the conventional elements of which he then used "slightly unconventionally" (Venturi, Scott Brown & Izenour 1977, 91).

It is also interesting that Venturi would rather talk about the richness of meaning rather than the clarity of meaning, preferring "both/and" to "either/or" (ibid., 16).

Venturi warns against oversimplification of architecture and describes his view on architecture as a combination of complexity and contradiction: "It (architecture of complexity and contradiction) must embody the difficult unity of inclusion rather than the easy unity of exclusion. More is not less" (ibid., 16).

Venturi and his companions created two concepts that should be explained: "the duck" and "the decorated shed". In the category of "ducks", they included mainly Modernist buildings, but also medieval cathedrals, where "the architectural systems of space, structure, and program are submerged and distorted by an overall symbolic form" (ibid., 87). The term duck comes from Peter Blake's book *God's Own Junkyard*, which included a picture of a duck-shaped commercial building. The entire building symbolises a drive-in restaurant, where one was very likely able to eat duck.

"A decorated shed" is a building "where systems of space and structure are directly at the service of program, and ornament is applied independently of them" (ibid., 87). Examples of this kind of architecture are the commercial buildings with their gigantic signs that flank the main streets in Las Vegas.

According to Venturi, many Modernist buildings have an expressive, heroic appearance but an ugly and ordinary interior, whereas Postmodern architecture uses ugly and ordinary materials but involves decoration that makes unconventional use of ordinary elements (ibid., 87). These small transitions and playful changes are the features that make Postmodern buildings *the architects'* "decorated sheds", and not architecture made without architects.

Since this chapter deals with ornamentation, it is interesting that the writers conclude that Modernist architecture rejects symbolism and underlines expressive features, focusing on the power of expression in the architectural elements themselves. According to Venturi, the building – a duck – becomes an ornament: "Ironically, the Modern architecture of today, while rejecting explicit symbolism and frivolous appliqué ornament, has distorted the whole building into one big ornament. In substituting "articulation" for decoration, it has become a duck" (ibid., 103).

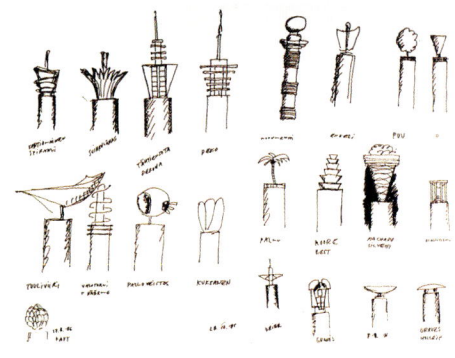

Jyrki Tasa: *BePOP* shopping centre, Pori, 1989. Picture: Jyrki Tasa.

Ornamentation in the postmodernist spirit. Jyrki Tasa: *BePOP* shopping centre, Pori, 1989.

Jyrki Tasa: sketches for the capitals of the columns. *BePOP* shopping centre, Pori, 1989.

In my opinion Postmodernism, as an architectural style, was fumbling after an ornamental expression, but the results usually lacked deeper substance. It is not really sufficient to change the size and location of a fire station's windows and place a sign on top of the entrance that reads *Fire Station 4*, as Venturi did (Robert Venturi, *Fire Station No. 4*, 1965–7, Columbus, Indiana).

The tradition had already been disrupted. Art Deco and Classicism in the 1920^s were the last styles to use abundant ornamentation successfully and with awareness of tradition. This did not, however, prevent Postmodernism from creating a number of interesting buildings. The *BePOP* shopping centre in Pori is a fine yet understated example of this in Finland. Architect Jyrki Tasa used a strong bent form that sweeps through the entire block, and the walls feature many fascinating details and colours. But there is no narrative that would give the building substance and a backbone. The ornaments are merely play with forms and colours, albeit effective play.

Jyrki Tasa made a speech about the *BePOP* centre in one of my seminars (at Erkki Pitkäranta's office on 13 April 2002), in which he commented on the Postmodern method of appealing to "the man on the street" while building for fellow architects, and the double coding this involves: pure lines and interesting structural divisions for colleagues, and ornamental details for the masses. Tasa wanted to find a balanced level of abstraction in the ornamental design in order to avoid slipping into kitsch and thus being susceptible to his colleagues' criticism. He tests, yet never crosses, the unspoken boundary that divides architecture from non-architecture.

The self-censorship that many architects practise is interesting. In the drafts for the pillar tops, Tasa displays a brisk sense of humour that he plays with and employs to make a statement about architecture's history and nature. Unfortunately none of this is present in the finished building. Perhaps the self-censorship took over, or was the deadline too tight? Or could it be that there is no room for playfulness in "serious" architecture?

The pillars at the impressive portal are, though, a sort of abstract synthesis of the drafts.

What happened to the joy of creating?

What is the essence of what was restricted and suppressed during the period of Modernism? I think it could be expressed in one concept: the joy of creating.

Even though it cannot be said that Modernists were lacking in creativity when they designed buildings, I think what mattered was the method, where simplification and exclusion were the core principles.

Destroyed ornamentation. The demolition of *The Blue House* (Carl Armfelt, 1902) in Turku, 2011

Ornamentation to create a spiritual space. Jan-Erik Andersson (in cooperation with architect Erkki Pitkäranta): *The River by the Mountain*, a total work of art integrated in the architecture. Masala Lutheran Church, Kirkkonummi, 2000.

The Masala church is an example of the kind of collaboration where Erkki and I haven't planned the whole building together. Pitkäranta was in charge of the building and I have planned the artwork. The artwork was planned at the same time as the building and was able to be included in the constructional drawings of the building, and therefore be funded as a part of the ordinary building costs.

In his article *Functionalism today*, the philosopher Theodor Adorno accuses Adolf Loos (with whom we began our argument) of rejecting joy and eroticism. Adorno thinks that Loos's absolute rejection of style becomes a style, and he says that Loos traced ornament back to erotic symbols. He links Loos's rejection of ornaments with his disgust with erotic symbolism (Adorno 1997, 10).

Adorno refers to Loos's writing *Ornament und Verbrechen*, where Loos claims the cross to be a symbol of sexual intercourse: the horizontal line presents the woman and the vertical line the man who penetrates her. According to Adorno, Loos seems to see the mimetic impulse in ornament, which runs contrary to rational objectification; he sees in it an expression that, even in sadness and lament, is related to the pleasure principle (ibid., 10).

Loos sees ornament as connected to pointless work and wasting of material, but Adorno argues that many things produced in today's (capitalist) society only pretend to be functional and useful. In fact, they are produced for profit's sake, and they satisfy human needs only incidentally. They call forth new needs and maintain them according to the profit motive (ibid., 17).

I'm inclined to agree with Adorno's criticism. Could the joy artisans feel after managing to bend their material to obey their will and to shape wonderful forms and structures be wasted energy? In many projects Erkki Pitkäranta and I have executed together, we have learned that the opposite is true. For instance, when the floor of the Masala Lutheran Church was put together from hundreds of different computer-cut pieces of tile, we would sometimes find the tiler busy at work late at night. Despite the numerous overtime hours, he later thanked us for the commission. His joy of overcoming the challenge and creating something unique was palpable.

Ornament today

Architectural discourse in the 21st century has dealt with green construction and, above all, buildings' exterior forms. Architects have discovered that CAD tools allow them to create buildings that become sculptures or that can, as Venturi said, be seen as ornaments.

Farshid Moussavi writes in *The Function of Ornament* that the strict regulations concerning a building's interior (storage spaces, server rooms, etc.) are the reason why an architect's role has been restricted to designing the outer shell. Other designers are responsible for the interior. The building's expression can be independent from the interior, yet it needs to contribute to the urban setting (Moussavi 2006, 5–6).

Moussavi talks about an ornamental surface but argues that symbolic ornaments no longer work: "It is clear that in a multicultural and increasingly cosmopolitan society, symbolic communication is harder to enact as it is difficult to gain a consensus on symbols or icons" (ibid., 6)."
Moussavi provides examples of buildings, most of which were built in this century, with façades that are expressive. It is telling that Moussavi avoids mentioning the term ornament and uses the concept "affect" instead.

In contrast to Postmodernism, Moussavi speaks for the kind of ornaments that appear to grow organically from the building materials. In her opinion, this is the reason they will retain their appropriateness over time.

> *It is through ornament that material transmits affects. Ornament is therefore necessary and inseparable from the object. It is not a mask determined a priori to create specific meaning (as in Postmodernism), even though it does contribute to contingent or involuntary signification (a characteristic of all forms). It has no intention to decorate, and there is in it no hidden meaning. At the best of times, ornament becomes an "empty sign" capable of generating an unlimited number of resonances (ibid., 8).*

The contemporary ornaments that Moussavi favours need to symbolise the (material) technology of the time so that the affects produce a seamless continuity with the Modernist concept of ornament, where the term is understood in a broader sense. Moussavi also separates ornament, which in her opinion is organically related to architectural elements and, with them, produces a so-called "affect", from decoration, which is something glued on: "Decoration is contingent and produces 'communication' and resemblance. Ornament is necessary and produces affects and resonance" (ibid., 8).

Moussavi's views show how heated architectural debate can become. There is little or no room for playfulness, contradictions or opposing views; everything must be thoroughly considered and consistent. But whatever Moussavi says about integrated ornaments, very few of her examples prove that the affects are in any way necessary to the structure of the building. As she says: "these buildings produce affects that *seem* to grow directly from matter itself" (ibid., 7).

Moussavi can, however, appreciate ornament's significance to the landscape. This is how she describes the affect of Norman Foster's *Gherkin* in London (image on page 29):

> *The 30 St Mary Axe office tower introduces a diagonal ventilation system, a diagrid, and two colors of glasses to contribute a spiral effect to the form. None of these specific decisions are crucial to the operation of the building interior, but they are vital to the affects they trigger in the urban landscape (ibid., 9).*

Mechanical structure as ornament. Jean Nouvel: *Torre Agbar*, Barcelona, 2005.

Small LED-lit glass panels react to changes in outdoor light and reduce the energy used for the air conditioning. Photo: Wikimedia Commons.

Sol LeWitt: *Kubus*, 1984.

Ornamentation to create a spiritual space. The portal of York Cathedral, ca. 1472.

Clean surface in art and architecture

Why am I so attracted to older, ornamented buildings? Why do I not find whitewashed building volumes or contemporary ornamentation; stylish abstract grids or double façades, equally pleasing?

I do not have a problem with minimalist art; no, I can appreciate Ellsworth Kelly's meditative "pure" paintings or Sol LeWitt's white block structures at a museum or gallery. But in a city, I find it hard to approach the kind of architecture that is naked of traditional elements of ornament and art, the elements that refer to the world beyond architecture. A clean surface on a building mainly brings out a sense of emptiness and a lack of something. It does not create a background for thoughts and imagination, but instead appears to be an empty abyss.

In order to better understand this "lack", I would like to introduce the philosopher Jacques Derrida (1930-2004) to this study. Derrida often refers to the concept of "abyss" in his book *The Truth in Painting* (1978), which deals with a frame's meaning in relation to a work of art. His analysis of "lack" might increase my understanding of my feelings.

The frame's meaning to Derrida and Kant

Risking oversimplification, I would describe Derrida's method as deconstruction of the ideal of "total presence in itself". This is the ideal of Western thought, according to Derrida, separate from the definitions of truth and meaning. For instance: Think about something true. "2+2=4". The meaning of that expression remains what it is, identical to itself, at all times, in all places, for all people. It does not differ from itself. Equally, if an individual could express perfectly what they feel and what they think, in full transparency, that would be an image of truth, truth as truthfulness.

Derrida contends that this ideal is precisely just that: something that can help approximate an understanding of meaning and truth, but that is never possible. It is a grave error to confuse an ideal and reality. Realistically, there is always another something in what seems the most self-identical, a relation to, for example: something else, to time, other people, materiality, etc.

"Différance" is an important concept for Derrida. It refers to the insight that in everything that is supposed to be completely present/identical to itself, the essential (the deepest meaning of the concept, a person's nature, the essence of a work of art) is, actually, what it is because of an addition, something else, a supplement. Anything that is ideally identical with itself, present in itself (meaning, truth, beauty, essence, substance) actually differs from itself.

This is Derrida's premise when he approaches the frame (parergon) and its relation to a work (of art) (ergon) that it is supposed to emphasise. Without the frame, the work is – and will always be – incomplete.

I will use this reasoning to support my interpretation that when traditional ornamentation was rejected, with the help of Modernist ideology, and it was thought that this would result in more complete and purer architecture, what was actually removed was the element that makes the entire building stand out, and so the building was left incomplete. In my opinion, giving the role of ornament to a material's surface pattern makes no difference.

Derrida provides an example of when there is something lacking inside: because reason is conscious of its impotence to satisfy its moral need, it has recourse to the parergon, to grace, to mystery, to miracles. It needs this

Ornament as a creator of a sensual and meditative space. Vilho Halmekari: *Loven Bohatus*. Halmekari whittled wooden panels, light fixtures and furniture over a period of 30 years, using a small knife. His intention was to make a whole building with these elements, but the project was never finished. A room was constructed out of the material he left behind for the *WILD – Fantasy and Architecture* exhibition (Turku City Art Museum, 2007). Photo: Vesa Aaltonen.

Ornament as a creator of a sensual and meditative space. The private chamber of Ahmed III in the Topkapi Palace. The room was also called the Fruit Room and was probably used for dining. Early 18th century.

Ornament as a part of the structure. The Roof window in the Dolmabahce Palace, Istanbul, 1856.

Ornamentation of a temporary shelter for pedestrians. Photographed in Helsinki 2007.

Sculpture as an ornament. The New Hermitage, St Petersburg, 1839-51.

Accidental ornamentation as a part of the construction. Photographed in the Kakola Prison in Turku, 2005. (No longer in use)

supplement. This additive, to be sure, is threatening and its use is critical. It involves a risk: to each parergon of religion there is corresponding damage. For grace it is fanaticism, for a miracle it is superstition, for the belief in the supernatural order it is illuminism and for the supernatural it is thaumaturgy. The parergon, thus, must be added because of reason's lacking inside (Derrida 1987, 56).

When discussing the frame's relationship to the work, Derrida goes back to Kant's views about ornament. To Kant, ornament is an adjunct, not an intrinsic constituent in the complete representation of the object. It can only affect the object's external beauty, and then only by means of its form. This applies to the frames of pictures, the drapery of statues and the colonnades of palaces. However, if the ornamentation has no beauty in itself, if it does not itself enter into the composition of the beautiful form (Kant offers a gold frame as an example: there merely to invite us to look at the painting), it only disturbs the experience of genuine beauty (ibid., 53).

A pure judgment of taste cannot be based on such sense or charm. I could add here in parentheses that Kant was more relaxed in his judgment of beauty in ornament compared to that in architecture, which, according to him, was restricted to remaining an object with a particular purpose (such as living) and could not be seen as separate from the other functions.

Derrida continues examining Kant by questioning the limits of the frame and the work; according to Kant, clothing on statues has the function of both a parergon and an ornament. But where does a parergon begin and end? A naked body is what is presented, the essence. Derrida, however, wonders if G-strings are also a parergon. Or a dagger that is held against a body to cover certain parts? Or a transparent veil that covers a naked body, if we bring a painting into the equation? What is it that is lacking in the representation of the body so that the garment should come and supplement it? (Ibid., 57–58)

Why does Kant think that columns are external to the building itself? Derrida maintains that a parergon is added to an object that does not represent anything and is itself already added to nature. We think we know what properly belongs or does not belong to the human body, what is detached or not detached from it, even though the parergon is precisely an ill-detachable detachment.

Derrida poses more questions: does a window form part of the inside of a building or not? What about the window of a building in a painting? What about the houses around buildings? They are not parerga, nor is the site, but columns are. But if columns are detached, the lack on the inside appears. What constitutes them as parerga is not simply their exteriority as a surplus, it is the internal structural link that rivets them to the lack in the interior of the ergon. Without this lack, the ergon would have no need of a parergon. The ergon's lack is the lack of a parergon (ibid., 61).

How can one assimilate the function of a frame to that of a garment on a statue, and to that of columns around a building; and what about a frame framing a painting representing a building surrounded by columns in clothed human form? (Ibid., 60)

A parergon has a thickness. The frame has two surfaces, one towards the inside, to ergon, and one towards the outside, towards the surrounding space. It stands out but not in the same way as the ergon. When it deploys its greatest energy, i.e. has the viewer focusing on what is inside the frame, it melts away. The frame is in no case a background in the way that the milieu or the work can be, but neither is its thickness as margin a figure (ibid., 61).

In order to be able to make an aesthetic judgment, Kant says we must distinguish intrinsic, true beauty from finery and surrounds. Derrida, however, points out the difficulty in distinguishing the frame (decoration) from the work (ibid., 63).

A parergon's double function can be seen; in Derrida's interpretation, Kant's frame can contribute to the aesthetic experience only through its form. If it has a beautiful form, it is part of the experience of beauty. A frame that is not beautiful, on the other hand, removes the experience of beauty. Derrida sees this as analogous to the four damaging elements of religion discussed above.

He continues to comment on Kant: even a gilded frame is detrimental to our pure aesthetic judgment. The colour has no form but is a sensory matter and can thus seduce us. As a design, organisation of lines and forming angles, the frame is not at all an adornment and one cannot do without it. But in its purity, it ought to remain colourless, deprived of all empirical sensory materiality (ibid., 64).

Lack inside a building

Interpreting Derrida very freely, I would like argue that the "lack inside" a building calls for ornamentation, or that a building, through its expressive form, becomes an ornament by its nature. We can verify this by studying architecture's history, where ornamentation played an important part until the 20th century. This view supports my experience of "yearning" that I feel when I see Modernist buildings that are inadequately ornamented or not ornamented at all.

A building's traditional ornamentation thus forms a kind of a frame, "an edge of abyss", which has both a concrete and psychological thickness. I claim, indeed, that ornament is the element (of art) that makes the building stand out and invites us inside.

Kant's views about ornamentation are also rather interesting. He says that Greek delineations and foliage for borders and wallpapers are free beauties (as opposed to natural beauties such as flowers). This distinguishes ornamentation from architecture, for example, which he links to its function, which "disturbs" the experience of beauty (Kant 2000, 81).

Derrida continues his interpretation of Kant: these structures (ornaments) are beautiful in the same way as art and free "wandering" beauties are, and they can give rise to a judgment of pure taste. They should not signify anything, represent anything, and they are deprived of theme and text. These structures can represent and signify, but they are freely wandering beauties only by not doing so. A building is finite in a way that man decides it to be. Even if its function as an apartment or a church comes to an end, it will retain an expression of the function it was designed for. Its beauty, thus, is not free but adherent – unlike the motifs on the wallpaper! (Derrida 1987, 97).

Derrida asks if the parergon constitutes the place and the structure of free beauty. What is left if we take away from painting all representation, all signification, any theme and any text-as-meaning, removing from it also all the material (canvas, paint) which, according to Kant, cannot be beautiful for itself? If we efface any design oriented by a determinable end, subtract the wall-background, its social, historical, economic and political supports what it left? The frame! (Ibid., 97–98).

Derrida tries to find a hole in Kant's reasoning: when Kant talks about "free beauties", he does not refer to the frame but to the motifs and foliage on the wallpaper. To Kant, the frame is linked to the work of art. According to Derrida, however, we could see free beauty as including a parergon too, as it is a-signifying and a-representative. Free beauty could manifest itself there just as well.

Derrida asks if there is a connection between free beauties and dependent beauties. We talk about the same beauty in both cases, so there must well be an adherence somewhere between the two (ibid., 100).

Ornament as a part of the structure: Apartment building in Greenwich Village, New York, 2005.

Recycled materials such as rope, glass and coal used as ornament. The pieces of glass incorporated in the wall can be seen both from the outside and the inside. Bruce Goff: *Ford House*, 1947-50, Aurora, Illinois.

A building as an ornament

If we approach ornamentation from, say, Kent Bloomer's point of view, it is difficult to consider an entire building as a form of ornamentation. Bloomer sees ornamentation as an art form in itself, governed by detailed rules (see p. 126). If, however, we decide to approach the issue from a point of view where art is also considered as a form of ornamentation, we may come to a different conclusion.

The philosopher Gianni Vattimo presents an interesting view about the term ornament. He questions the concept of art. According to him, all art is a kind of ornamentation because it is "weak thought" as opposed to "strong thought" represented by "reason". He prefers to see ornament in all art, and is backed up by his interpretation of Heidegger. When all art is peripheral, there is no point discussing ornament's peripheral position (Vattimo 1997, 158). This applies to contemporary art in particular, as it typically draws attention to the peripheral issues and events and brings them to the forefront of our attention. Architecture is in a special position because it includes all other forms of art (a concert hall provides an arena for music and poetry, a museum for visual arts, a city for environmental art, and so on), but as it has been said, a building's function is to draw attention towards life.

Heidegger says that art emerges at the moment when truth steps forward (ibid., 157). Artwork is capable of bringing out something essential. He gives the example of a Greek temple, which through its essence makes us see, for example, the flowers growing in front of its façade from a fresh viewpoint. The temple brings out the flowers. The temple achieves this by being a temple-work.

But what brings the building out? I argue that only an art element fitted in/on the building can bring the building out, to make it bloom. This point applies, above all, to ornament, which has a double function: to first draw people's attention to the building itself, and then take it away from the ornamentation back to the building and what can be done in it. We could follow Vattimo and take a step further and pay attention to the life surrounding the building. Thus the building as a whole becomes an ornament.

The philosopher Hans-Georg Gadamer's thoughts on art are similar to Vattimo's. He thinks architecture is the highest art form. Architecture gives shape to space. Space is what surrounds everything that exists in space. That is why architecture embraces all the other forms of representation: all works of plastic art, all ornament. Moreover, to the representational arts of poetry, music, acting and dancing it gives their place. By embracing all the arts, it everywhere asserts its own perspective. That perspective is: decoration (Gadamer 1997, 135).

Gadamer wants to review the traditional dichotomy between "a real work of art" and "what is only decorative". He wants us to keep in mind that in their original meaning, the ornamental and the decorative were the beautiful as such. Ornament is determined by its relation to what it decorates, by what carries it. Even Kant said, when talking about tattoos, that ornament is ornament only if it suits the wearer. Ornament is not primarily something by itself that is then applied to something else, but rather belongs to the self-presentation of its wearer. Ornament is part of the presentation, but presentation is representation. An ornament, a decoration, a piece of sculpture set up in a chosen place are representative in the same sense that, say, the church in which they are to be found is itself representative.

The building as a whole turning into an ornament. In addition, wooden shingles have also been used as an ornamental feature both inside and outside the building. Olavi Koponen: *Gastropod*, private home, Espoo, 2006.

Leftover wood used as an ornate surface as well as to create a pattern for the roof overhang. Rosegarden Art & Architecure (Jan-Erik Andersson and Erkki Pitkäranta): *Cumin*, ecological cow shed, Teuva, 1997.

Ornamentation created by Kent Bloomer on the Chicago Public Library, designed by Thomas Beeby, 1991.

Ornamentation to create a spiritual space. Mimar Sinan: Rüstem Pasha mosque, Istanbul, 1561.

Ornament with a function. Walking map for the visually disabled on the floor of Kamppi bus station, Helsinki. Photographed in 2005.

Ornate entrance for a public playground in Leeds. Photographed in 2003.

Ornamentation with functional elements, Sibiu, Romania. Photographed in 2007.

Ornamentation with pictures. Sigge Architects, Pekka Mäki and Reijo Suomi, Turku, 2012.

Concrete shape ornaments. Photo taken outside Bremen railway station in 2007.

Ornamentation as a continuation of nature. Ödön Lechner: Postal Savings Bank, Budapest (1899–1902).

Surface, structure, ornament

Art historian Anne-Marie Sankovitch seeks support from Derrida to show how ornamentation is an organic part of a building's structure.

In her article in *The Art Bulletin*, she writes that it was only in the 19th century that a building began to be seen in terms of dichotomy, as a structure with attached ornament (which was the feature that defined the building's style). At the same time, there was a request that the building be of a uniform style. Sankovitch writes about how the Church of St Eustache in Paris (1532–1640) has been described over time.

After the building was completed, people admired its grand interior, the great quantity and variety of its sculptural decoration, the great height of its vaults and so on. This attitude did not change until the 19th century, when the influential architect and theorist Viollet-le-Duc described the church as sort of Gothic skeleton. He said it was draped in Roman rags sewn together like the pieces of a harlequin's costume. Ever since critics have agreed that the building is a mixture of styles. All contemporary commentators agree on the duality between structure and ornament even if their interpretations vary, but most of them, however, are annoyed about the church's "lack of style".

Maurius Vachon, though, found a positive angle in 1910. He wrote that St Eustache has the boldness and majesty of construction of the great cathedrals of the Middle Ages. It has the fantasy, the grace and the elegance of sculptural ornamentation of the civic monuments of the 16th century. We can see that Vachon replaced Viollet-le-Duc's "Roman rags" with "elegant sculptural fantasy".

I would highlight the word *fantasy* here, a word seldom used in architectural discourse.

Sankovitch points out that on closer look at the structure/ornament pair of concepts, we can see that "structure" may have two meanings. Firstly, it can signify the actual technical structure, the material realisation of the tectonic principle by which load, support, and thrust are accommodated or, secondly, the entire structure, the complete work of architecture itself, which has an ornamental part, and can be used as a synonym to terms "building" or "monument". Ornament is often considered as an accessory, to be attached to the structure, as a fragment detached from the structure, that can be, at most, a memory. The structure may also be trivialised as something invisible that can only become visible when all ornamentation is removed. Ornament can be considered an element that reveals and makes present structure by pointing to and compensating for what structure lacks. Sankovitch talks about wholeness, which is only achieved when ornament appears on the scene. She, too, leans on Derrida, who says the lack of the interior of the work of art (ergon) is the reason it requires the supplement (parergon) to become whole. Therefore it is not easy to point out where ornament ends and structure begins.

St Eustache is perceived to be a Gothic church with Renaissance ornamentation. The ornamentation is the only clearly visible feature, but we cannot remove it or see through it without destroying the structure. They are both are there, says Sankovitch, but they do not coexist in the simple oppositional way that so many modern texts would have us believe.

Sankovitch also shows that structure can be seen as an abstract and metaphorical design (governing concept and essential idea) that informs everything else. In this case, ornament is necessary so that the structure can gain physical presence. The entire built building becomes the ornament.

St-Eustache, Paris, (1532–1640). Photo: Wikimedia Commons, David Monniaux, 2006.

Márta Nagy's contemporary ornamentation using classic Zolnay ceramics in the lobby of the library building in Pécs. Building designed by Török és Balázs Építészeti, 2010.

Mikko Heikkinen/Markku Komonen/Markku Puumala: The County Archives in Hämeenlinna. Aimo Katajamäki designed the ornamentation on the facade, 2009.

Ilmari Lahdelma and team: Maritime Centre *Vellamo*, 2009. The building itself is like an ornament, while the facade is ornamented with both abstract colour fields and figurative prints, 2008.

Inside and outside

For the entire 20th century, architectural discourse used the structure/ornament pair in a way that defined them as separate entities, so that either structure is considered as aesthetically and ethically pure "Kernform", or the Postmodernist way of building "decorated sheds" rather than architectural "ducks" (p. 134). Of course there have been architects such as Frank Lloyd Wright who tried to combine structure and ornament.

We should, however, keep in mind that before the 1900^s, structure/ornament were not understood to be separate concepts, as even Sankovitch showed us. Structure was not understood to be an entity with a self-sufficient ontological, representational or aesthetic presence, and ornament was not conceived as a discrete, detachable object. Sankovitch mentions Alberti (1404–72), who for instance, said: "The chief ornament in every object is that it should be free of all that is unseemly." For Alberti ornament could be anything from a column or the leaves on a Corinthian capital to empty spaces in the surface of a wall, the quality of the material and a building's relative proportions or the relationship between its component parts. Which means he included elements the contemporary discourse considers to belong to the structure.

Ornament's role in today's architectural discourse concerns the question of what the load-bearing structure (the functional, actual framework) has in common with the (ornamented) exterior that communicates with the outside world by covering, pointing to or emphasising the building's construction.

The philosopher Sven-Olof Wallenstein tackled this question in his book *Den moderna arkitekturens filosofier*. He mentions archaeologist Karl Bötticher's (1806–89) book *Die Tektonik der Hellenen* (1844–52). According to Bötticher, the Greeks could recognise an inner "juncture, or joining" (Junktur) between a "shell" and "core". For this reason style was a necessary expression for them. An architectural form is based on the "body-form" (Körperbild), where internal and external become one the same way as nature and construction organically become one in the concept of "techne".

Against the internal Kernform (core form), there is the external Kunstform (art form) as an aesthetic expression. It is unnecessary in architectural tems, but its function is to show the core in the "expressed" manner. We can thus define "tectonics" as that which elevates construction to art (Wallenstein 2004, 24). Wallenstein writes that this is lacking in the modern; in other words, the connection, con-juncture, that connects the internal and external to a sort of supplementary movement (ibid., 24).

The idea was further developed by others, Adolf Göller (1846–1902) among them. Wallenstein refers to one of Göller's lectures (given in 1887): Göller maintains that external "style case" (Stilhulse) must express the internal core, make it attractive and concrete. Truth cannot be defined through a representational system, but through direct faithfulness, through expressiveness that connects the internal and the external by showing the art form's structural elements. In architecture, it deals with the relations between the building's structural forces, the material's texture and so forth (ibid., 24–25).

Wallenstein is, though, doubtful about this rhetoric:

> Yet there is a gnawing doubt that this materialist expressiveness is just rhetoric like its predecessors, that, irrespective of whether it is about representational systems or the structure's material quality, truth is always interaction between what we see and what is covered, and that all metaphors that we use to describe this relation will inevitably be ambiguous (ibid., 25).

Wallenstein then moves to the architect Gottfried Semper's (1803–79) theory of "Bekleidung". Semper talks about a building's shell as "dressing". He plays with associations concerning "Wand" (wall, screen) and "Gewand" (dress, clothing). Textile is ornamental and veiling, and to Semper it denotes the "screen" element rather than a technical function, which he links with "wall" (Mauer); ibid., 25).

Clothing covers the structure whilst emphasising it; brings it out by reminding that it is behind everything, interacting between that which defines (shell, dressing) and that which is being defined (body, structure) (ibid., 25).

Semper stresses that architecture came about as a result of advances in technology and not so much because of reflections on ideal forms. It might be interesting to mention here that Semper was one of the first to advocate the pureness of materials. He wants bricks to look like bricks, timber to look like timber and iron like iron. Yet he defended multi-coloured architecture with a particular reference to Northern Europe. He says: "Colours are less harsh than the daxaling white of our stuccoed walls" and asks: "Are our fields, our forests, our flowers grey and white? Are they not far brighter than in the south?" (Kruft 1994, 311).

> As professor Fritz Neumeyer points out, the concept of tectonic has always been suspended between what we see and what we know. Seeing has its own legitimacy, its own history that does not always keep pace with the development of constructive thinking. The tectonic deals more with the image of structure than structure itself, and when the image detaches from its "juncture", it becomes freer as the reference to the truth of the body in background becomes weaker (Wallenstein 2004, 26).

Ornamentation with bolts without a function. Otto Wagner: Postsparkasse in Wienna, 1906. Photos: Wikimedia Commons.

Ornamentation with I-beams without a function. Ludwig Mies van der Rohe: Seagram Building, New York, 1957. Photo: Wikimedia Commons.

Ornate entrance. Native American home. The entrance is under the beak of the pelican. The Canadian Museum of Civilization, Ottawa. Photo taken in 2002.

Vilho Penttilä: The Wilkman Building, 1904.

As we have seen in previous chapters, Modernist theories about how a building's shell, art form, must develop from the structure did not quite materialise in the way Modernist architects acted in reality. Wallenstein, too, recognises this and introduces the architect Otto Wagner (1841–1918) as an example. The aluminium plates on the façade of *Postsparkasse* in Vienna (1904–6) are not attached to the structure with the 15,000 big iron bolts that attracted so much attention when the building was completed, but with small screws. The bolts are an ornamental element (ibid.).

Perhaps the most famous example is Mies van der Rohe's Seagram building (1958) in New York. Mies van der Rohe was one of the leading post-war architects and advanced the minimalist architecture of steel and glass to new heights. The I-beams that were so typical of his designs are visible on the exterior. They do not have any function other than suggesting the structure inside; they are ornamental. The load-bearing I-beams are invisible inside a fire-proof structure behind the ornamental beams. Robert Venturi comments on them:

> *Less may have been more, but the I-section on Mies van der Rohe´s fire resistant columns for example, is as complexly ornamental as the applied pilaster on the Renaissance pier or the incised shaft in the Gothic pier. (In fact, less was more work) (Venturi 1997, 114).*

Conclusion about ornaments

Every example mentioned in this chapter proves that ornamental surface, art form, does not need to be drawn from the building's structure. We could say it shares internal similarities with the structural construction. This view is supported by philosophers like Derrida, yet it mostly acts as a symbolic storeroom. Ornamental surface is a symbolic storeroom that can very well symbolise technology. This was the case for the Modernist movement but it could just as easily symbolise something else, nature for instance.

I would like to point out that a building requires well-designed and well-executed ornamentation in order to feel cosy and to stand out as energetically as possible. There are not any functional or moral laws, however, that stipulate that we must ornament our houses in a particular way, or that the ornamentation should refer to the structural elements, for example.

Taking a broad view of ornamentation, we can even perceive a Modernist pure surface as ornamental if the architect chooses a material with an expressive pattern. It has also emerged that minimalist surface is not necessarily cheaper. How we experience the shell's aesthetics is a matter of taste and has nothing to do with an absolute judgment of beauty. Modernism is a style amongst other styles. We have also found support for the idea that a building as whole can be considered an ornament.

Finally, I would like to comment on Moussavi's claim that representative iconography is not valid in a multicultural society, where frameworks are very different and change all the time. I think that this claim is one of the many that have tried to prove Modernism's excellence using ostensibly universal arguments.

We can easily widen today's range of ornaments so that we could ornament our houses with hobgoblins, fairies, camels, dragons, polar bears, palm leaves, coffee cups, spades and hearts; the majority of the world's population might even understand these better than a building ornamented with Mies van der Rohe's I-beams. Fairy tales, stories and fantasies are, just like geometric elements, universally accessible. Just think how popular Tolkien, Philip Pullman and J.K. Rowling are all over the world. Our mental health needs fantasy! And not fantasy shut off in some theme park but as part of our everyday environment.

I cannot see any firm evidence to prove that a geometric world is on a higher level than the real and representational world. The abstract geometric level may just as well be considered a lower level that is needed to bring harmony and beauty to a work of art, but by adding representational elements on top of the geometric structure, we can reach even higher.

Johan Victor Strömberg: Kuopio market hall, 1902.

Next spread: The facade of the Leaf factory in Turku photographed in 2006. The factory, which produces sweets, moved its production abroad the same year.

The Illinois Institute of Technology campus building in Chicago (2003) by Rem Koolhaas creates an "iconic space". Koolhaas integrated the old and noisy "L" line into the building, which is full of amusing details, gently playing with Mies van der Rohe, whose classic building is next to the campus. Mies van der Rohe's ornamental face is by graphic designer Michael Rock and consists of small simplistic human figures.

DIARY

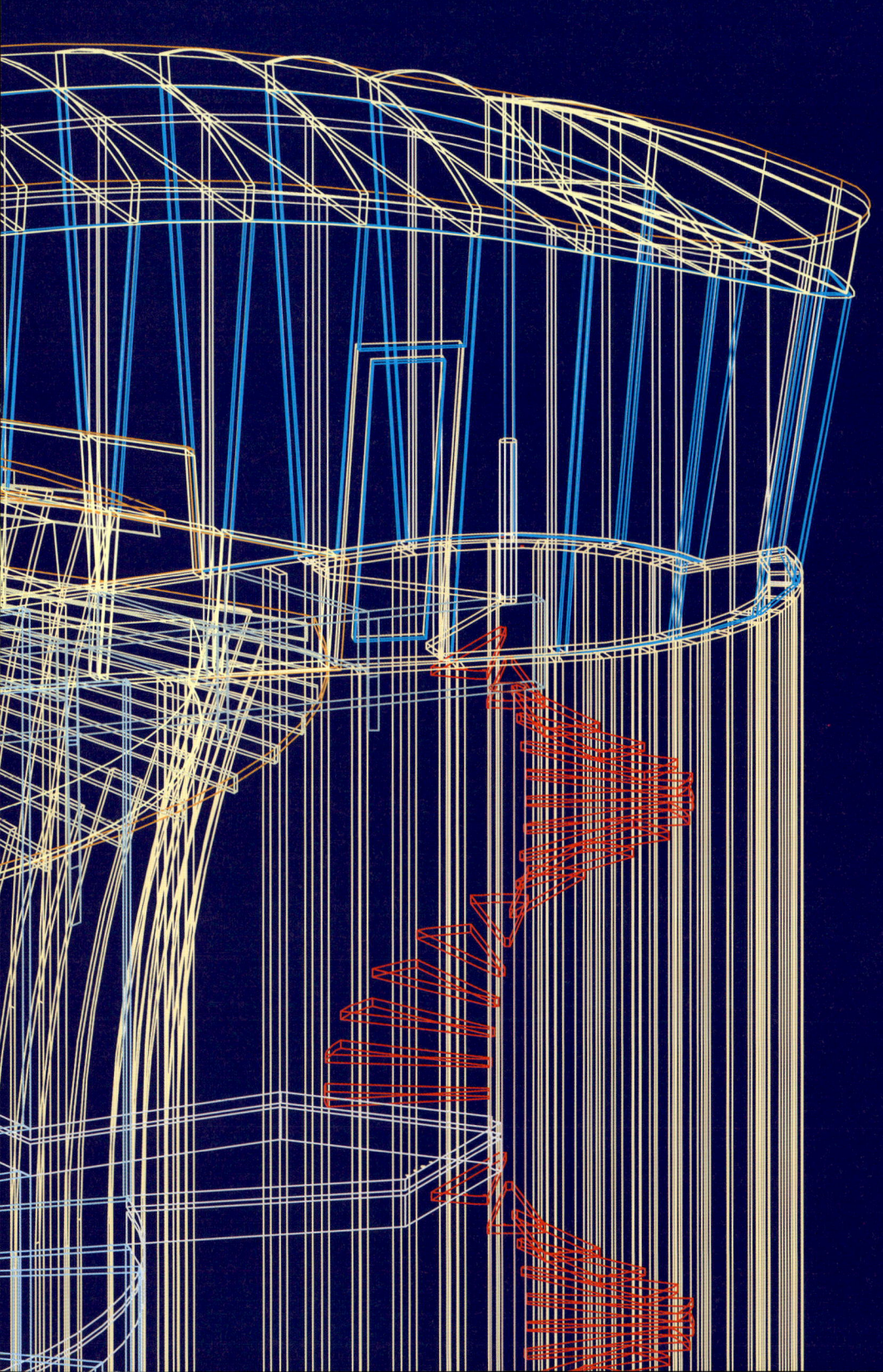

"One must live to build one's house, and not build one's house to live in."

Gaston Bachelard, 1958

2001–2004

2005

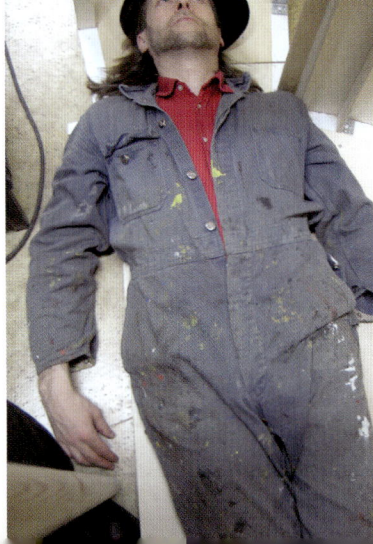

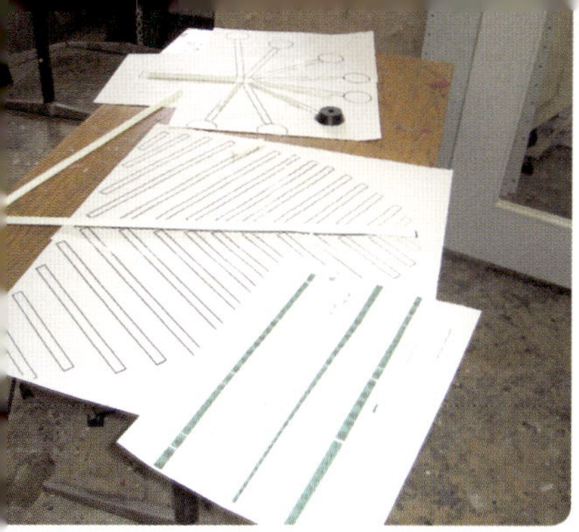

2006

2007

2008

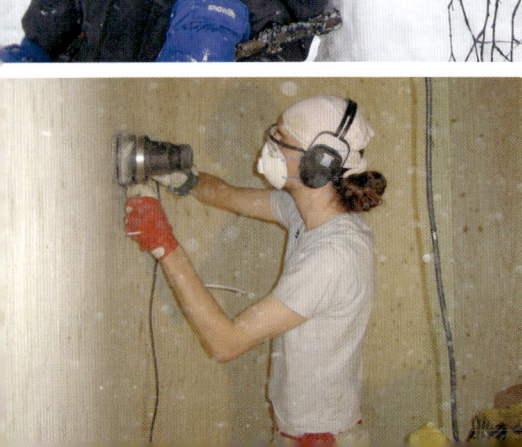

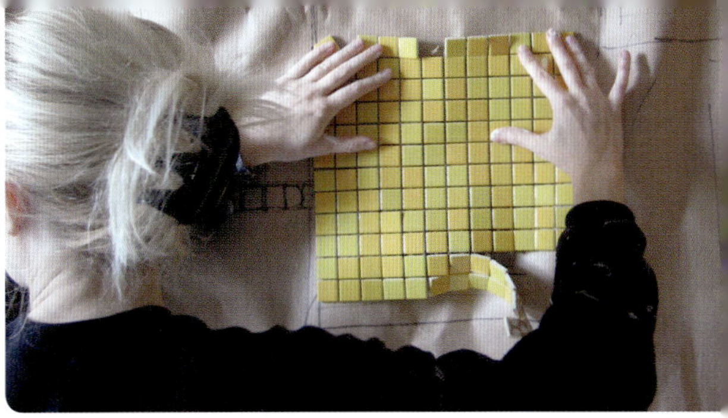

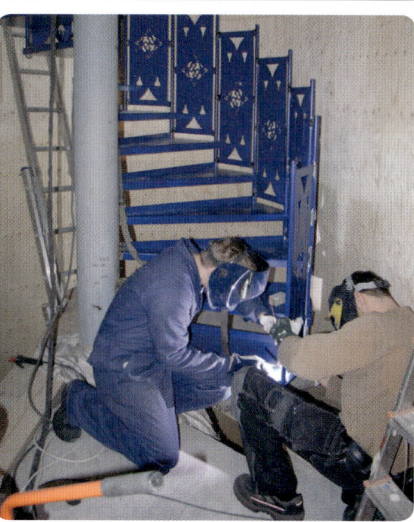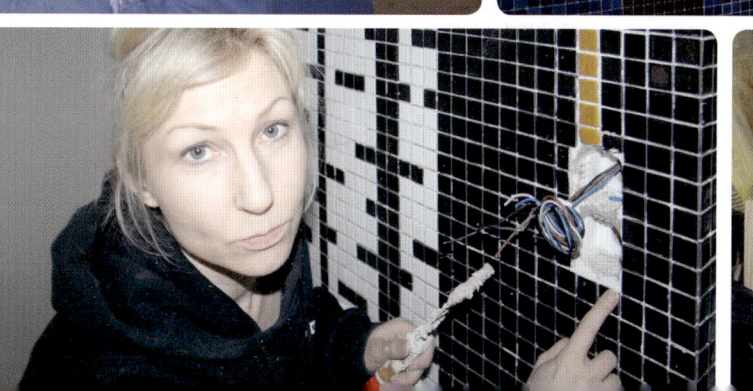

2009

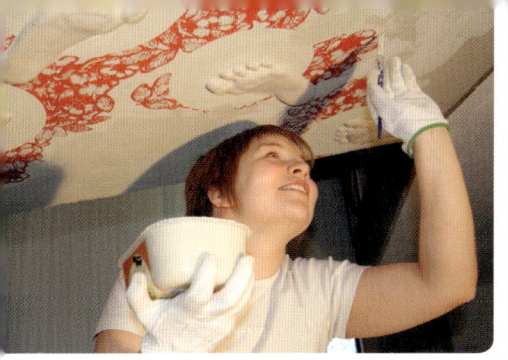

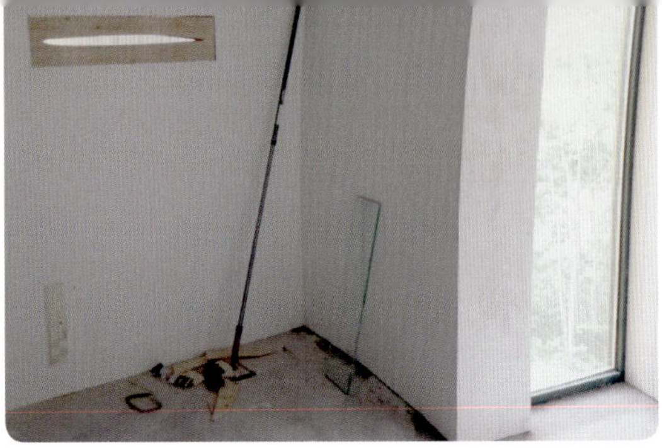

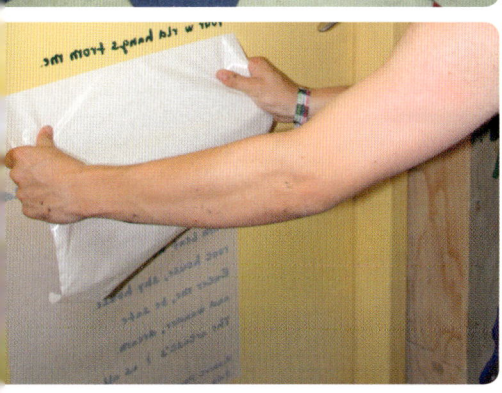

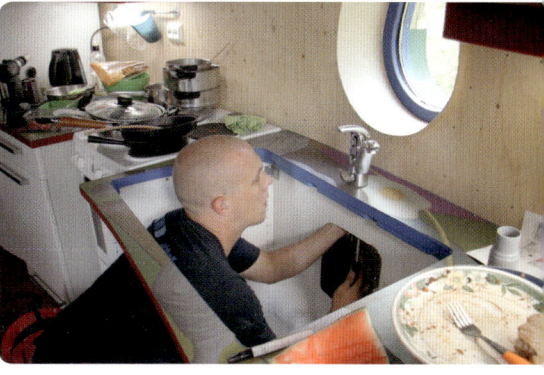

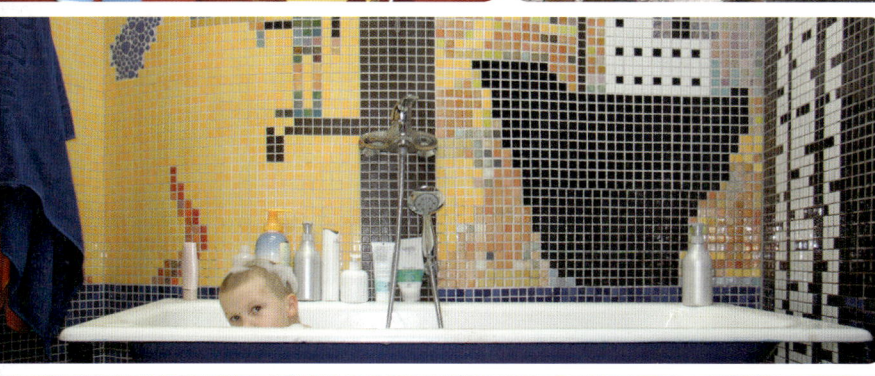

Technical Information

The house is heated by geo-thermal heat. A 170 metre deep hole is drilled into the rock from which energy is retrieved. The thermal heat pump is situated in the small outbuilding of the *Life on a Leaf* house, which also functions as a storage space. The outbuilding, also benefiting from the heat pump, doubles as a laundry room.

The heat is delivered to the main building by a system of pipes containing the heated water, embedded in the concrete floors. Most of the windows are sealed and the air circulation is mechanically driven by a system which transfers the heat from the outgoing air to the incoming air.

The building is founded on pillars. Under the supporting concrete platform is a 150 mm thick layer of Polystyrene. On the platform is a 50 mm thick layer of Polystyrene and a 80 mm thick layer of concrete, which holds the pipes for the heating system. The stiffening structure between the ground floor and the first floor is reinforced concrete and the pillars steel and concrete.

The structure inside the outer walls are seven metre long 200 x 51 mm Glulam wooden beams, made in the shape of the walls, which are curved both horizontally and vertically. The insulation inside the walls is a 200 mm thick layer of natural thermal insulation, which is made of recycled newspaper. On the outside there is a 25 mm thick drywall made of wood fibres, fastened on the Glulam beams. Linen insulation is used to insulate the window and door profiles.

The bearing structures of the roof and the Bluebell winter garden are also Glulam beams. The inner roof is made by a layer of 39 mm thick plywood sheets. Insulation is the same as in the walls, thickness 400 mm. Almost all the windows are made of sealed triple pane glass elements.

The "bell shaped" structure of the house is also good for energy efficiency because the ratio of the surface of the outer core compared to the volume remains small. The percentage of the surface area of windows to the whole facade area is 12.7 %. The Bluebell winter garden is not taken in account, because it is not heated to room temperature the whole year around.

Symbolically the interior design of the 147 m^2 house points out the importance of recycling and reuse. All the wash basins, toilet stools and the bath tub are from recycle centres. The family's old furniture is reused; the living room sofa covered with a new fabric, designed by an artist.

Invited artists

Trudi Entwistle (Hebden Bridge, UK)
Apple Heart

Benches/sculptures outside the house.
Design of the earth mounding around the house.
www.trudientwistle.com

Frank Brümmel (Turku)
Bee Dance

Stone paving with ornate pattern outside the front door and concrete outdoor table.
www.frankbrummel.com

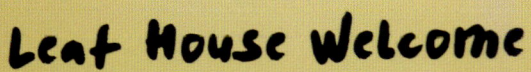

Robert Powell (Wakefield, UK)
Leaf House

A welcome poem on the entrance door.
Read: www.anderssonart.com/leaf

Jan-Kenneth Weckman (Turku)
Hot Lines

Drawing on the surface of the heat preserving owen
www.jankennethweckman.fi

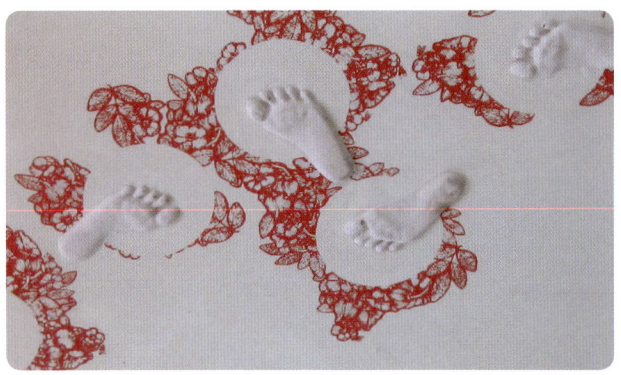

Susanna Peijari (Turku)
The Dance

A relief/painting under the bridge crossing the living room.

Johanna Kunelius (Saint Petersburg)
The Lions on the Sofa and The Lion and the Leaf.

Textile patterns for the sofa and pillows in the living room.
www.johannakunelius.com

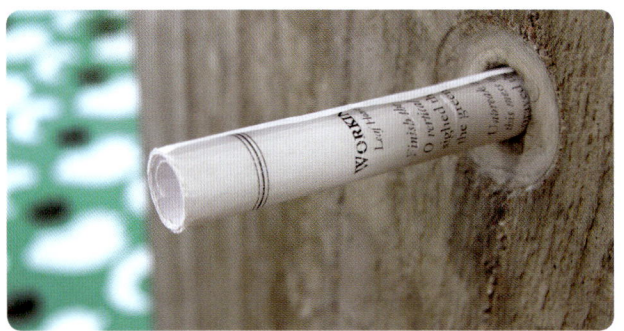

Alice George (Chicago)
Working Play Song

Poem on a roll of paper to be found in a hole in the concrete wall in the kitchen.
www.alicegeorge.org

Pertti Toikkanen (Järvenpää)
Wheat Hat

Light fixture in the kitchen

Kari Juutilainen (Kuopio)
The Cleaner

Light fixture in the kitchen
personal.inet.fi/taide/kari.juutilainen

Karin Andersen (Bologna)
Science Kitchen

A digital image for the kitchen working table surface.
www.karinandersen.com

Burtonwood & Holmes (Chicago)
Apache

Wallpaper pattern for the toilet on the first floor.
www.burtonwoodandholmes.com

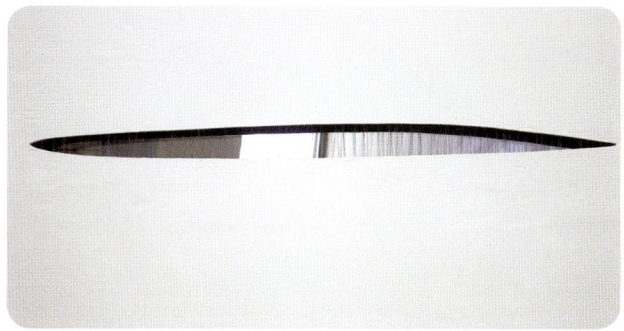

Yuichiro Nishizawa (New York)
Fir tree needle

A hole through the wall shaped like a fir tree needle.
www.liminalspace.org

Pierre St-Jacques (New York)
Grand Central Station

Video which can be seen through cut out in the floor of the second floor.
www.pierrestjacques.com

Jyrki Siukonen (Tampere)
Stuttering Modernist Shit

Collage made for the toilet wall.

Shawn Decker (Chicago)
Sound Bridge

Sound work for the railing on the bridge inside the living room. Outdoor changes in wind and light affect the sound.
www.shawndecker.com

Leah Oates (New York)

Printed photographs from the Transitory Space Series.
www.leahoates.com

Amy Youngs & Kenneth Rinaldo (Columbus Ohio)

Sprout House

Proposal for a sprout growing lamp.
www.kenrinaldo.com

Eileen Hutton (USA/Ireland)

Blue Tit Nest #10

2010 Nesting Season

The Burren, Co. Clare, Ireland.

N 53° 2.6723208'

W 8° 57.787628'

Sculpture made in collaboration with the birds, hanging in the Bluebell winter garden.
www.eileenhutton.com

Ismo Kajander (Helsinki/Paris)

Pea pod-sandbox

Proposal for a sandbox for children.
www.kajander.net

Joonas Mikola (Rovaniemi)

Buxo Birdhouse (Yellow)

3D graffiti. Hanging from a tree outside the house.
joonasmikola.blogspot.fi

Karin Andersen: *Science Kitchen*, detail.

Rosegarden Art & Architecture
Jan-Erik Andersson, Erkki Pitkäranta, www.rosegarden.fi

Gerbera 1998, gardening school, Janakkala, Finland

The house takes its form from Gerbera, which is grown in the school's greenhouses. Classrooms are under its petals and there is a winter garden in the middle.

The winter garden was inspired by a story about the 13th century alchemist Ericus Kipulensis, who created the first genetically manipulated birch tree. The students work on three leaves that came from this tree, placed on top of the ruins of Kipulensis's laboratory.

Here, sound artist Shawn Decker produced the first public sound installation in Finland that utilises the sounds of birds, the wind, the rain and silence recorded in the surroundings by the sound artist Simo Alitalo.

Cumin 1997, eco-friendly cowshed, Teuva, Finland

An environmentally-friendly cowshed for 50 cows, designed on cows' terms, shaped like a cumin seed because cows simply love wild cumin. "A piece of yellow cheese", the bulls' "lounge", is stuck into the side of the building.

Cows are social animals. They can move around freely and find their own space around the oval-shaped area where calves stay. Since cows like being in a forest, one was made for them from old telephone poles, which also support the roof. The entire cowshed was made of recycled materials, and there is even a skylight, made of recycled greenhouse plastic, so that the cows can admire the stars at night.

The solution for heat insulation is simple: the cows grow a thicker fur when it gets cold. This allows them to exercise outdoors even in the wintertime!

Jan-Erik Andersson:

From the Iconic Space series: *Hidden in the Prow*. Photographic triptych, 2012. Chromaluxe metal print.

Life on a Leaf -Video kiosk Installation.
The roof and the walls of the kiosk are made of materials left over from the construction period.
– Video from the construction of the house (2006–2009).
– Video with glimpses of the life in the house (2010).
– Realtime webcam image from the house. Gallery VISU, Kokkola, 2014.
Kaarisilta Art Gallery, Helsinki, 2012; *ECO Art*, Pori Art Museum 2011 *Momentum Design – art, design and the space in between*, Punkt ø, Moss, Norja (Galeri F15), 2010. *Living Space – an Unusual Experience*, Laznia Centre for Contemporary Art, Gdansk. 2010, *Rakentajat – Taiteen talot ja tilat*, Kuopio Art Museum, 2010, Serlachius Art Museum, 2010.

Life on a Leaf – Video installation.
Presenting the house as artistic research in the *Personal Structures* exhibition, Palazzo Bembo, Venice Biennale, 2013.
– Video from the construction of the house (2006–2009).
– Video with glimpses of the life in the house (2010).
– The book about the house project, translated into English, as a PDF document on two iPads.

Life on a Leaf construction table
Pictures from the construction period glued onto leftover building materials. Interactive installation. ECO Art, Pori Art Museum, 2011. *Living Space – an Unusual Experience*, Laznia Centre for Contemporary Art, Gdansk, 2010.

References

Adorno, T. (1997). Functionalism Today. In N.Leach (Ed.) *Rethinking Architecture. A reader in cultural theory*. (pp. 6–19). London: Routledge.

Alison, J. (2010). The Surreal House, London: Yale University Press.

Alsop, W. (2004). We need imaginative approaches. People making places. Imagination in the Public Realm. Wakefield, UK: Public Arts publication.

Ando, T. (1996). Towards New Horizons in Architecture. In K.Nesbitt (Ed.) *Theorizing a New Agenda for Architecture. An Anthology of Architectural Theory 1965–1995* (pp. 456–461). New York: Princeton Architectural Press. Original work published 1991.

Antoniades, A.C. (1992). *Poetics of Architecture*. New York: John Wiley & Sons.

Bachelard, G. (1979). On Poetic Imagination and Reverie. Woodstock, Connecticut:Spring Publication.

Bachelard, G. (1958/1994). The Poetics of Space. (M. Jolas. Trans.). Boston: Beacon Press Books.

Beskow, E. (1930/2002). *Hattstugan* (The Children of Hat Cottage),. Bonnier Carlsen bokförlag. Originalutgåva 1930.

Beskow, E. (1932/n.d.). Branden i Fläderköping. In *Landet Långthärifrån* (The Land of Long Ago).

Blair, s. & Bloom, J. (2004). Islamic Ornament. In M. Hattstein & P. Delius (Ed.) *Islam. Art and Architecture*. (pp.124–127). Tandem Verlag GmBH. Originaltitel: Islam. Kunst und Architektur 2004

Bloomer, K. (2000). The Nature of Ornament. *Rythm and Metamorphosis in Architecture*. New York: W.W.Norton & Company.

Brolin, B. (2000). *Architectural Ornament. Banishment & Return*. New York: W.W. Norton & Company.

Collins, J. (2007). *Sculpture Today*. London: Phaidon Press Limited.

Colomina, B. (1994). *Privacy and Publicity. Modern Architecture as Mass Media*. Cambridge: MIT Press.

Cornell, P. (1981). *Den hemliga källan. Om initiationsmönster i konst, litteratur och politik*. Gidlunds.

Derrida, J. (1987). The Truth in Painting. (G. Bennington, I. McLeod. Trans.). Chicago: The University of Chicago Press.

Escritt, S. (2000). *Art Nouveau*. London: Phaidon Press Limited.

Foster, H. (2011). The Art–Architecture Complex,. London: Verso.

Friedman, A. (1996). Domestic Differences: Edith Farnsworth, Mies van der Rohe, and the Gendered Body. I C. Reed (Ed.) *Not at Home* (pp. 179–192). London: Thames & Hudson.

Gadamer, H–G. (1997). The Ontological Foundation of the Occasional and the Decorative. In N.Leach (Ed.) *Rethinking Architecture. A reader in cultural theory*. (pp. 126–137). London:Routledge.

Gombrich, E. (1979). *The Sense of Order. A study in the psychology of decorative art*. London: Phaidon.

Hausen, M. (2000). In Pallasmaa, J. (Ed.) *Hvitträsk. Koti taideteoksena*. (pp.10–67). Keuruu: Otavan kirjapaino Oy.

Hawthorne, C. 2013. Review: Stedelijk Museum's 'bathtub' awash in awkwardness. http://articles.latimes.com/2012/sep/28/entertainment/la-et-cm-stedelijk-expansion-20120929Printed 25.4.2013.

Hayes, A. & Moon, S. (1990). *Ragdale. A History and a Guide*. Berkeley: Open Books.

Herwitz, D. (1993). Making Theory/Constructing Art:On the Authority of the Avant-Garde. *Chicago : University of Chicago Press.*

Hunter, I. (2007). Merzbau Kiihdytetty arkkitehtuuri-Kurt Schwittersin Merz-rakennelmat. In Andersson J-E & Budney J. *WILD – Fantasia ja arkkitehtuuri*. Helsinki: Maahenki.

Isozaki, A. (1995). Introduction. I K. Karatani. *Architecture as Methaphore. Language, Number, Money*. (pp. vii–xiii). London: The MIT Press.

Jencks, C. (2005). *The Iconic Building*. London: Frances Lincoln Ltd.

Jenger, J. (1996). *Le Corbusier Architect of a New Age*, London: Thames and Hudson.

Kandinsky, W. (1912/1981) *Taiteen henkisestä sisällöstä*. Helsinki: Suomen taiteilijaseura ry.

Kant, I. (1790/2000). *The Critique of Judgement*. (J.H. Bernard. Trans.). New York: Prometheus Books.

Kimmelman, K. (2013). *Why Is This Museum Shaped Like a Tub?* www.nytimes.com/2012/12/24/arts/design/amsterdams-new-stedelijk-museum.html?_r=0 Printed 25.4.2013.

Kruft, H-W. (1994). *A History of Architectural Theory. From Vitruvius to the Present*. New York: Princeton Architectural Press.

Lahuerta, J. J. (2003). *Casa Batlló. Gaudí*. Barcelona: Triangle Postals.

Le Corbusier (1931/1986). *Towards a New Architecture*. (F. Etchells. Trans.). New York: Dover publications.

Lever, M. (2006). Marie Antoinette. The Last Queen of France. London: Portrait.

Liungman, C. G. (1974/1994). *Dictionary of Symbols*. W.W. New York: Norton & Company. Orginalutgåva 1974.

Loos, A. (1908) Ornament and Crime. In I. Frank (Ed.) *The Theory of Decorative Art*. (pp. 288–294). New Haven: Yale University Press.

Loze, F. & Loze, P. (1991). *Belgium Art Nouveau. From Victor Horta to Antoine Pompe*. Gent: Snoeck-Ducajun & Zoon.

Menin, S. & Samuel, F. (2003). *Nature and Space: Aalto and Le Corbusier*. London: Routledge.

Moorhouse, J. (1998). *Helsingin Jugendkorttelit, kävelyretkiä*. Helsinki: Kustannusyhtiö Taide.

Moussavi, F. (2006). *The Function of Ornament*. In F. Moussavi & M. Kubo (Ed.) The Function of Ornament. (pp. 5–11). Harvard: Actar.

Nyman, Kaj, letter 17.8.2000.

Paaso, J. (2008). Nykyaika–vuonna 2008. *Arkkitehtuuriuutiset 3/2008* (pp. 14–15)

Pallasmaa J. Opponent statement concerning Jan-Erik Andersson's *doctoral degree at the Finnish Academy of Fine Arts:* Life on a Leaf –Iconic Space. My house as an architectural artwork. Academy of Fine Arts ,Helsinki. 8.11.2008

Rand, H. (1993). *Hundertwasser*. Köln: Tashen.

Reed, C. (1996). Introduction. I C. Reed (Ed.) *Not at Home* (pp. 7–17 London: Thames & Hudson.

Ringbom, S. (1986). Transcending the Visible: The Generation of the Abstract Pioneers. I E. Weisberger (Ed.) *The Spiritual in Art*. New York (pp. 131–153). New York: Abbeville Press.

Sankovitch, A-M (1998). Structure/ornament and the modern figuration of architecture. *Art Bulletin*, The, *Dec, 1998*. Retrieved December 18, 2005, from http://findarticles.com/p/articles/mi_m0422/is_4_80/ai_54073966?tag=artBody;col1

Sharr, A. (2007). *Heidegger for Architects*. New York: Routledge.

Sullivan, L. (1892). Ornament in Architecture. In I. Frank (Ed.) *The Theory of Decorative Art*. (pp. 284–287). New Haven: Yale University Press.

Tanner, M. (1995). Wagner, Richard. In D. Cooper (Ed.) *A Companion to Aesthetics*. (pp. 439–441). Oxford: Blackwell Publishers Inc.

Trilling, J. (2003) *Ornament. A Modern Perpective*. Seattle: University of Washington Press.

Vattimo, G. (1997). Ornament/Monument. In N.Leach (Ed.) *Rethinking Architecture. A reader in cultural theory*. (pp. 155–160). London: Routledge.

Venturi, R. (1977). *Complexity and Contradiction in Architecture*. Original from1962. New York: The Museum of Modern Art.

Venturi, R. & Scott Brown, D. & Izenour, S (1977). *Learning from Las Vegas*. Revised edition. Original from 1972. Cambridge: MIT Press.

Vesely, D. (2010). The Surrealist House as a Labyrinth and Metaphor of Creativity. S.41. Jane Alison ed. The Surreal House, London: Yale University Press.

Vitruvius. (2009). On Architecture. London: Penguin. The original work probably from the first century B.C .

Wallenstein, S-O. (2004). *Den moderna arkitekturens filosofier.* Stockholm: Alfabeta bokförlag.

Wertheim, M. (1998). The Medieval Return of Cyberspace. (pp. 47–59). In J. Beckmann (Ed.) *The Virtual Dimension. Architecture, Representation, and Crash Culture.* New York: Princeton Architectural Press.

Widler A. (2000). Warped Space, Cambridge, Massachusetts :The MIT Press (Second printing 2001)